At Home with God

By the same author

**Homely Love: Prayers and Reflections Using
the Words of Julian of Norwich**

An armchair retreat guide for everyone who must 'make do' spiritually in one way or another, inspired by Julian of Norwich who chose a simple, confined life.

[Penny Roker] ... 'writes with a simplicity, clarity and conviction',
New Directions

978-1-85311-733-6

www.canterburypress.co.uk

At Home with God

*How to go on retreat without going away
– a programme and guide*

Penny Roker RSM

CANTERBURY
PRESS
Norwich

© Penny Roker 2009

First published in 2009 by the Canterbury Press Norwich
Editorial office
13–17 Long Lane,
London, EC1A 9PN, UK

Canterbury Press is an imprint of Hymns Ancient and Modern Ltd
(a registered charity)
St Mary's Works, St Mary's Plain,
Norwich, NR3 3BH, UK

www.scm-canterburypress.co.uk

Scripture quotations are from the Good News Bible published by
The Bible Societies/HarperCollins Publishers Ltd UK © American
Bible Society, 1966, 1971, 1976, 1992.

British Library Cataloguing in Publication data
A catalogue record for this book is available
from the British Library

978 1 85311 995 8

Typeset by Regent Typesetting, London
Printed and bound in Great Britain by
CPI Bookmarque, Croydon, Surrey

Then you will call to me. You will come and pray to me, and I will answer you. You will seek me, and you will find me because you will seek me with all your heart. Yes, I say, you will find me . . .

Jeremiah 29.12–14

Contents

Introduction

Making a retreat at home

Everyone seems to be searching for something these days. Even people of faith may feel that God is elusive at times. We are all reaching out in one way or another. This book learns from the experience of the ordinary – and not so ordinary – men and women we read about in the Gospels. Like them, we will find that God is not far off but within our reach, and where better to reach out to God than from our homes, the place where we are most ourselves? It may surprise us to discover that, in reaching out to God, we will also find meaning, peace, belonging, identity, friendship and all those other things for which people are busy searching. Seek, Jesus reassures us, and you *will* find.

The Gospels tell us about people who did exactly that: some travelled many miles; some waited through the years; some recovered a lost faith; others needed help to recognize who or what they were looking for. All the time, Jesus was treading the dusty roads of Palestine, in search of hearts and homes where he might find a welcome . . . we are not the ones who initiate the search. Each chapter of this book reflects on a different Gospel character who reached out to a God who first reached out to us. We will recognize ourselves in their stories.

What prompted you to take this book from the shelf? Was it a desire for more space in your life, a time to rest and take stock? That too is within reach. Jesus regularly sought 'time apart'. He looked for solitude in wilderness places. Some would say that it is essential for us, as he did, to get right away. Unfortunately, travel to a retreat centre may not be possible for those who lack the necessary energy, finances, independence or mobility. There are also other reasons why people feel they cannot go away on retreat. Fear may present a formidable barrier to anyone who doubts their own capacity for periods of silence, sharing or introspection: you may want a 'home trial' before committing yourself to anything more. Quiet time at home can only be second-best to a retreat away, but if it is time that is consciously set aside as a trysting place with God, then God will surely honour it and meet you there.

Retreats are not meant to be an endurance test: people usually respond to a warm and pleasant environment where the 'work' of prayer and reflection are fuelled by good food and balanced with exercise. 'Being with God' need not be all serious. You may choose to go walking or even sight-seeing, though an important element of being on retreat is learning to be alone. An enjoyable trip to town with friends might be therapeutic in its own way, but avoiding the 'pain barrier' of unaccustomed solitude makes it less likely that you will gain insights about how God is working within you. Even music can be unhelpful if it is just another way of filling the emptiness. For this reason most retreats encourage silence, solitude and a 'short rein'. A complete break from your usual activities and routines is important. You need to slow down in order to notice the things you do not normally have time to notice, in both the world about you as well as the world within.

This, then, is a book for anyone who recognizes the need for a short period of withdrawal from responsibilities and the distractions of everyday life in order to focus on self-care and spiritual growth. A retreat at home requires more preparation than at a retreat centre where everything is laid on: gardens, walks, chapel, retreat directors, and full board. We cannot replicate all that. Given a little forethought and planning, however, a less stressful environment than normal is achievable within the home setting – unless, that is, you are a full-time carer or have young children. If there are always other people in the house, you may be able to find somewhere within daily travelling distance. Failing that, a weekly or monthly quiet day, even an hour or two during the day if the children go to school, might be built in. Unexpected 'home alone' opportunities may arise from time to time when you can recharge your batteries for a couple of days and just 'be'.

Using the book

There is ample material in this book for anything up to an eight-day retreat, though it is unlikely that such a long period of uninterrupted quiet can be sustained in the home environment. It is more likely that it will be a two- or three-day retreat at home, followed by some quiet days now and then. Though the 15 chapters are designed to be taken in sequence, it may be that you will prefer to select those with more immediate personal appeal. Some chapters are appropriate for particular times of the church year, such as Chapters 10–15, suitable for Lent. Each chapter is intended to occupy a half or whole day. It is recommended that you do not move through the book too quickly: reflective reading is about 'chewing' rather than 'gobbling'. You do not have to use the book as a retreat: for busy people who do not have whole days or even whole hours to spare, any of the reflections, prayers and suggested activities may be used with the scripture reading for short 'quiet times'.

Slowly read the scripture once or twice, then the reflection, before setting aside half an hour or so to ponder on the questions. It is unnecessary to reflect on them all, as long as at least one of them 'takes you somewhere'. You will probably need a longish break after that to absorb this work of reflection. It often happens that some real insight will come to you when you are not expecting it, so do not rush on to the next chapter too quickly. It will be important to bring any insights, issues or questions that may have arisen into a time of prayer, when you can articulate your feelings, struggles, thanks or requests to God. You may want to use words or just remain in silent trust and adoration. The litany and suggestions for intercessory prayer might be part of this prayer time.

There are other ways of expressing yourself using, for example, art or dance or song. On retreat you can be free to experiment and let yourself go. At some part of the day you might need to do something physical or practical, and the 'Activities to consider' sections offer suggestions. Some of these involve visiting people or using the internet: if you have resolved to seek complete solitude during this time of retreat, it would be wise to postpone these for the time being.

The book lends itself to group work, such as a Lenten study course, or for gospel-sharing. The suggested activities would combine with quiet reflection time to make a balanced timetable for a parish Quiet Day. The questions for individual reflection could be followed by group sharing, and the litany and intercessory prayers provide the structure for a worshipful response. Responses are in bold print for use in a group. A hymn or chorus could be slotted in. Although the questions for reflection are not suitable for children, some of the activities lend themselves to whole-family involvement.

Preparing yourself for a retreat at home

For a private retreat of some days, you will need to plan ahead. Whereas at a retreat centre the boundaries are already in place, at home you will have to make arrangements for yourself. Here are some guidelines:

1 **Claim the time you need.** Mark the dates in your diary, consciously designating them well ahead so that you do not find yourself squeezing retreat time in – or out. If you feel that a retreat is a priority, then it is up to you to make it one. Do not be too ambitious, however. Most people start with a short retreat until they get used to solitude. Remember that at a retreat centre there are other people around even if they are not talking to you. A retreat on your own at home may seem very isolating. Undertaking a private retreat of any longer than a weekend when you have never made a retreat before is to set yourself up for failure. The book has enough chapters for you to start with a few quiet half-days, then to work up to a whole day until you feel ready to spend a longer period alone without distraction.

Free yourself from routine responsibilities within that period by, for example, making sure the house is clean, the lawn mowed, the shopping done, and other chores dealt with so that the days are not eroded by housework. You will need to decide in advance what to do if the telephone or doorbell rings, and to avoid or re-schedule appointments. If you go out or do things around the house, it must be because you want to, rather than because you have to. Explain to your close associates that you intend to spend this time in quiet and solitude, requesting that they refrain from calling or phoning except in emergencies. Let people know that you will not be contacting them between certain dates so that they are not concerned if they do not hear from you.

2 **Create a peaceful environment.** Jesus calmed the storm . . . now you try! Freedom from noise and distraction is really important. Short periods of quiet are good, but they are not equal to the full experience of a retreat where you 'grow into' silence until you begin to locate an inner sanctuary within yourself that you can carry into your normal life. You need to accustom yourself to quietness, especially if you are used to constant noise. Retreat centres make it easy for you: at home you must be self-disciplined.

Learning to be alone is the most important 'prayer space'. It may mean journeying through a wilderness of emptiness and loneliness, even a sense of futility, before the space feels inhabited by you in relationship with God. Then it starts to feel sacred. It is one thing to desire a de-cluttering of busy schedules and noisy chatter, but quite another to feel really at home in the echoing space left behind. The first day (and moments thereafter) may seem unbearably lonely, but moods pass and before long you will be moving more slowly and enjoying the tranquillity.

So think carefully about whether or how much you need the television, films, radio or newspapers during the retreat time: set yourself some rules and stick to them. Ideally you will not make any telephone calls. If there are other people in the house, it may be unreasonable to impose silence for any length of time, but you might discuss your needs with them and try to negotiate times in the day when the house is quiet and people leave you alone. If you manage to secure a silent environment, you will have done well. Distractions of your own making are likely to keep popping into your head, but do not be disappointed. The mind is accustomed to its preoccupations and takes time to settle down. The things that distract you may be telling you something about your needs, anxieties and compulsions. Take them to God in prayer instead of trying to banish thoughts. If you are going to banish anything for the duration of the retreat, make it your mobile phone and laptop.

3 **Find the right place.** You need a warm, comfortable, well-lit and ventilated place to read and to settle to the work of reflection. Find an upholstered chair with good back support that you like sitting in, and maybe a footstool. Have a rug handy in case you get chilly. You might need to experiment with various places around the house or garden until you find just the right spot. It is important to be able to see out and equally important not to feel overlooked.

You also need to provide yourself with a prayer focus, either here or in a different place. It will be somewhere specifically set apart for prayer for the duration of your retreat. It can be a table or wide windowsill. Enjoy creating this space. Assemble objects that feel special, such as a crucifix or cross, a candle and holy pictures or scenes from nature, and natural things like pebbles, leaves or seashells gathered from any walks you might take. Fresh flowers are always a help, and perhaps some water in an attractive bowl. Have a music player at hand with some CDs for special prayer times, but do not be tempted to use sound as 'wallpaper'. Involve your senses in creating the prayer space: fragrance, colour, beauty, texture, sound. Leave an empty 'today' space for any symbols, objects or drawings you come across or make during your retreat. Think about your prayer posture . . . will you need a different chair, a beanbag, a prayer stool?

4 **Make practical provisions.** Ensure that there is enough food, medication, etc. to make shopping trips unnecessary. This is not selfishness or escapism. You are on honeymoon with God. If you do not prepare ahead, then you will not feel free. As for your heart and mind, ask the Holy Spirit to prepare them in the days beforehand so that you are ready and full of anticipation. Just as in packing a suitcase you may need to take out some of the things that weigh it down, so recognize any elements of disquiet, self-righteousness or laziness creeping in. Voice them to God and ask him to help you remove them from your 'spiritual luggage'.

Some dos and don'ts

1 **Respect yourself.** Do not set unrealistic targets that make this a penance rather than a delight. It is not about endurance or one-upmanship, but about building a relationship between yourself and God. Keep things simple and relaxed. Move, eat, walk and get up more slowly than normal. There should be no set agendas. Treat yourself as God treats you: challengingly but within a context of forgiveness, complete acceptance, compassion, gentleness and patience. There is a fine line between serenity and boredom, so change activities regularly: reflecting, walking, creating, praying, resting, having a cup of coffee with your feet up, watching the sun set, and so on.

Eat and exercise sensibly. This is not an appropriate time to deprive your body of anything that it needs. Nor must you be busy reflecting or praying all the time: sketching, writing poems or your journal, taking photographs, bird watching, doing a jigsaw, are reflective activities that give you a break without detracting from the process of quietening down and slowing down. Beware of starting a book that you find difficult to put down: a compelling story will distract you from the on-going inner dialogue.

Do not fight your tiredness . . . give in to it and take naps. Care for yourself in other ways too. Periodic times of withdrawal or 'wilderness experiences' do not separate us from the body of Christ even for an instant. The Christian life is not a lone quest, but always within the teaching and fellowship of the Church. You may want to attend services as part of your retreat. Your local church may be the best place to seek appropriate support should you feel you need it. Beginning a private retreat is not really a good idea if you feel low; and if your retreat time raises painful issues that you feel you cannot handle on your own, then finding a spiritual director, church minister or counsellor with whom to talk things through would be sensible.

2 **Reverence God.** Do not treat your Lord and God with any less warmth or courtesy than you would treat anyone else. Remember that this time is more about listening than talking, but you might try to put into words what it is you desire from this retreat. Maybe *you* need to hear that more than God does.

Prepare for times of prayer or reflection by quietening yourself and lifting your heart to God in a conscious offering of all that you are. Listen to your breathing and slow it down. If it is something you are accustomed to doing, make the sign of the cross very deliberately at the beginning and conclusion of your sessions. At the ending of each session, remember to thank God for his gracious company. Be glad if you do not feel very holy: God is the holy one. You are at least honest and humble, so put yourself in his hands and feel loved instead.

Ending the retreat

Prepare to resume your everyday life with almost as much care as you took to embark upon your retreat. Do not rush back; if you can, take things at a gentler pace for a day or so. Think about what you are going to say to people who might ask how you got on or where you have been. You are under no obligation to disclose personal material unless you want to: making yourself vulnerable to teasing or ridicule may deaden God's message of love. You may want to write down any resolutions you decide to incorporate into your life, such as more regular prayer time, starting a reflective journal, going to bed earlier, or making some creative space for yourself.

What will I have discovered at the end of this retreat? Will God feel any closer? Will I be a different person? There is every chance that you will feel as though you have travelled a long way. Like any pilgrim, you may feel a longing to get back to normal life mixed with regret at having to relinquish the peace and quiet. You may feel that you are seeing the world through different eyes. Like pilgrims who discover on reaching their destination what they already knew back at home or deep within themselves, you did not have to make all this effort to find God; and yet, in some mysterious way, you needed the journey . . .

1

Within reach

... of the wise

Matthew 2.1–12

Jesus was born in the town of Bethlehem in Judaea, during the time when Herod was king. Soon afterwards, some men who studied the stars came from the east to Jerusalem and asked, 'Where is the baby born to be the king of the Jews? We saw his star when it came up in the east, and we have come to worship him.'

When King Herod heard about this, he was very upset, and so was everyone else in Jerusalem. He called together all the chief priests and the teachers of the Law and asked them, 'Where will the Messiah be born?'

'In the town of Bethlehem in Judaea,' they answered. 'For this is what the prophet wrote:

> *"Bethlehem in the land of Judah, you are by no means the least of the leading cities of Judah; for from you will come a leader who will guide my people Israel."'*

So Herod called the visitors from the east to a secret meeting and found out from them the exact time the star had appeared. Then he sent them to Bethlehem with these instructions: 'Go and make a careful search for the child, and when you find him, let me know, so that I too may go and worship him.'

And so they left, and on their way they saw the same star they had seen in the east. When they saw it, how happy they were, what joy was theirs! It went ahead of them until it stopped over the place where the child was. They went into the house, and when they saw the child with his mother Mary, they knelt down and worshipped him. They brought out their gifts of gold, frankincense, and myrrh, and presented them to him.

Then they returned to their country by another road, since God had warned them in a dream not to go back to Herod.

During my teenage years the Beatles blazed a trail to India on what they hoped would be a life-changing spiritual quest. They were followed by two of my more intrepid school friends in their 'gap year', leaving us less adventurous girls behind to work in Marks and Spencer throughout the long summer break before going to university. Hitch-hiking to India seemed the ultimate in exotic travel: it felt that the east stamped a seal of authenticity on mystical experience. As for me, stuck in the hosiery department, the answer to life looked likely to pass me by.

We look outside ourselves, beyond the familiar, for answers; we make spiritual journeys lengthier and more difficult than they need be. Pilgrimage is nevertheless a wonderfully enlightening Christian experience, one that other religions value too. There is something transforming about setting out into the unknown and committing oneself to God's providence. The dangers of travel symbolize our vulnerability in allowing God to challenge our thinking, shake us out of our comfort zone, and ask more of us than we can easily give. Away from the securities of home and status, it is easier to catch the sound of God's still, small but insistent voice. God dwells in mystery and we can only travel there by letting go of at least some of our certainty.

A retreat is like a pilgrimage. We do not have to travel miles in a geographical sense; we do need, however, to travel some distance cognitively. We need to open the eyes of our mind to fresh vistas. Old outlooks, received ideas and self-deceptions must be challenged and stretched. A retreat, even at home, must induce something of a pilgrim's insecurity and free us from the noisy distractions that make us 'poor reception areas' for God's gentle prompting. As the prophet Hosea said of his wayward wife, '*I am going to take her into the desert again; there I will win her back with words of love*' (Hosea 2.14). God leads us away from our comfort zones in order to win us back too.

The story of the Wise Men, such a well-loved part of the Christmas story, has captured the imagination of Christians throughout the ages. Their particular quest was to test an astrological prediction: that a new king of the Jews was about to be born. Not content to discuss his birth as an interesting phenomenon, their desire was to engage with it, at whatever personal cost. They stand as a challenge to anyone who claims to believe in Christ, but is not willing to go beyond intellectual assent. Wise men let faith disturb their routine. They were, in this sense, true pilgrims, for they did not expect to return home the same as they set out. Openness to change is the prerequisite for any spiritual journey.

The Wise Men possessed the necessary courage and humility to change, yet they were human too. Ignoring Micah's prophecy that the future leader of Israel would come from the little town of Bethlehem, they headed straight for Jerusalem to look for the new King of the Jews in the most obvious place

. . . a palace. We too must learn that Jesus waits for us in the places he feels most at home, and they are not necessarily the places we expect. Having failed to find directions in the city, the Wise Men did not give up. This time they trusted the star. God helped them to experience their world in a more attentive, spontaneous and wondering way.

The star led them to an ordinary house and there they found their royal baby. Luke's Gospel suggests that it was a stable and that he was actually lying in an animal's feeding trough. The Wise Men did not put their heads into the stable and turn away, thinking they had made a mistake. Overjoyed to be guided to this place, they 'brought out their gifts'. We can imagine them coping with whatever social embarrassments and language difficulties may have gone with this encounter of human beings from vastly different cultures. How sensitive they had become to God's prompting is shown by the serious attention they paid to a dream in which they were warned of Herod's hostile intent. Evidently they had opened to Jesus not just their treasures, but also their minds.

What we wish to see in Jesus is perhaps a projection of what we desire deep down for ourselves. We relish the idea of majesty and even more the idea of our association with it, rather as the sons of Zebedee did when they asked to sit at Jesus' right and left hand when he came into his glory. The Wise Men, however, even prior to setting out, seemed receptive to a different concept of kingship. Their gift of myrrh anticipated a suffering Saviour of his people. How prophetic they were, for this chapter at the beginning of Matthew is mirrored at the end of the Gospel by that other recognition of Jesus' kingship. The Roman soldiers guarding Jesus, also Gentiles, placed a crown upon his head, a scarlet robe about his shoulders, a makeshift sceptre in his hand and, just as the Wise Men had done three decades earlier, hailed him King of the Jews. But the crown was of thorns, not gold, and their homage was mockery. By this time in the Gospel story, the reader has come to realize, perhaps sadly, that the attributes of kingship were never in Jesus' earthly life to be external insignia.

What do *we* seek in King Jesus? Not pain or humiliation, surely. Yet to recognize Jesus as King is to understand that, just as all of us must experience these aspects of the human condition, Jesus shares his people's suffering. Jesus shows us how to find, not a way of avoiding life's troubles, but a way through them. He demonstrates by his kingly demeanour how to face scorn and rejection, how to carry heavy burdens, such as loneliness and physical agony. In King Herod the Wise Men encountered manipulative egocentric power; in the infant King, they found a different quality of leadership: solidarity with his people. It was with Jesus that they left their gifts.

The Church has always appreciated the significance of the Wise Men. Epiphany is the season after Christmas when we celebrate the revelation of God's salvation to non-Jewish peoples, represented by these eastern visitors. The good news of this message of love was announced to the whole earth. Christ's birth is good news for it is God's revelation of himself to us. The presence of God also brings self-revelation. That too is glad tidings.

The festival of Epiphany began the tradition of present-giving. The gifts of the Wise Men were heavy not just with material value, but also with symbolic value. Gold, representing wealth and status, recognized Christ's kingship. Frankincense, used ritually, acknowledged Christ's priestly role. Myrrh, a costly ointment for both healing and burial, anticipated Christ's suffering. Gold, frankincense and myrrh together symbolize the gifts we too must bring if we come in the true spirit of worship, for we must offer our whole selves to the Christ-child: our material possessions and bodily selves, our spiritual capacity and our readiness to follow Jesus to the cross. These we entrust into the hands of a baby and render ourselves as vulnerable as him.

Unlike gift-giving in our own homes at Christmas, there was no apparent reciprocity in the scriptural account of the Wise Men's visit. Mary and Joseph willingly welcomed them into the presence of their baby son, but offered no other exchange of gifts. Do we sometimes make sacrifices of time or money to the Christian cause in the hope of getting something back? We will be disappointed if the principal aim of our retreat is to feel better because of it. The Wise Men came to Bethlehem, not to benefit personally by their visit, but to pay homage. This too must be our purpose. We must lay aside any underlying agenda and say with the Wise Men: 'We have come to worship him.'

Personal Reflection Time

➤ The Wise Men were led by a star. What led me to make this retreat?

➤ What gift from me does Jesus desire?

➤ The Wise Men realized the danger of getting involved with Herod and avoided crossing his path again. What 'alternative route' might I need to take in my own lifestyle or relationships?

Prayer

> From far places of self-exile
> **I have come to worship**
>
> Across the wastes of past years
> **I have come to worship**
>
> Risking comfort and reputation
> **I have come to worship**
>
> Guided along the journey
> **I have come to worship**
>
> Bringing the treasure of myself
> **I have come to worship**

We remember before God . . .

- Those entrusted with prophetic wisdom

- Those entrusted with political power

- Those entrusted with the care of children

Activities to Consider

❖ Look up at the stars (as long as there is no cloud and you are not affected by light pollution). Be 'led' in your imagination.

❖ Return from your next journey by a less direct and more interesting route. If you normally walk or cycle, you might consider going more slowly in order to take in the scenery.

❖ Offer someone a gift that is meaningful to them. It doesn't have to be expensive.

2

Within reach

. . . of the lowly

Luke 2.8–20

There were some shepherds in that part of the country who were spending the night in the fields, taking care of their flocks. An angel of the Lord appeared to them, and the glory of the Lord shone over them. They were terribly afraid, but the angel said to them, 'Don't be afraid! I am here with good news for you, which will bring great joy to all the people. This very day in David's town your Saviour was born – Christ the Lord! And this is what will prove it to you: you will find a baby wrapped in strips of cloth and lying in a manger.'

Suddenly a great army of heaven's angels appeared with the angel, singing praises to God:

'Glory to God in the highest heaven, and peace on earth to those with whom he is pleased!'

When the angels went away from them into heaven, the shepherds said to one another, 'Let's go to Bethlehem and see this thing that has happened, which the Lord has told us.'

So they hurried off and found Mary and Joseph and saw

the baby lying in the manger. When the shepherds saw him,
they told them what the angel had said about the child.
All who heard it were amazed at what the shepherds said.
Mary remembered all these things and thought deeply about
them. The shepherds went back, singing praises to God for
all they had heard and seen; it had been just as the angel
had told them.

People throughout the centuries, from desert fathers to astronauts, have searched for God across vast expanses of sand or space. The shepherds found him close by. Out in the open, tending their sheep, they were unexpectedly treated to a vision of angels, before being invited into the sacred intimacy of the baby Jesus. In company with Mary and Joseph, these working men were privileged to see and touch the incarnate Son of God. Feelings of terror turned to joy as they praised God for the good news of his love for humankind, news that could be trusted because they had seen it for themselves.

If only *we* could apprehend God with our senses and say with St John, 'We write to you about the Word of life . . . We have heard it, and we have seen it with our eyes; yes, we have seen it, and our hands have touched it' (1 John 1.1). But we have not looked at or touched Jesus. We may no longer feel the same joy or excitement about his birth that we felt at Christmas-time as a child. If only I could reach up to heaven, we may think, or that God would reach down to me!

Perhaps that is how the shepherds felt as they huddled for warmth by night in the open fields, nervously watching for shadows of wolves, and looking up with wonder at the starry night sky. No one on earth could seem further from God in his highest heaven than first-century shepherds. Living with their animals on the margins of community life, they were probably considered unclean. Though we may not share ancient Jewish views about ritual cleanliness, we do still tend to look up to people or down on them according to their title, wealth, physical attributes, skills or respectability. God's scale of valuing is very different from ours. No one is more valuable to him than any other on grounds of usefulness or outward attraction. For him there is only the intrinsic value of all things because he created them, not randomly, not on a whim, but in love.

Luke uses the imagery of contrasts to demonstrate God's overturning of the criteria by which humans define importance. It was to the marginalized that God announced the sign of his favour; in a little town that God in the Highest came down as a human being; with men living rough that the heavenly host kept company; in the darkness of a sheep field that God's glory shone. The incarnation of God, if we take it seriously, overturns our sense of scale and value just as surely as Jesus would one day overturn the gold-stacked money-changers' tables in the Temple courtyard. What to us may seem a topsy-turvy viewpoint is seen in Jesus' teaching about the kingdom of God where the meek inherit the earth, where the rich man begs a drop of water from a beggar, and where the greatest must be servant of all. It comes as no surprise that God Almighty should choose to be incarnated as a poor man's child and that he should rest not in a canopied cot, but in an animal's feeding trough.

Mary's inspired song, the Magnificat (1.46–55), which Luke also records in his Gospel, has as its theme this same reversal of secular values: the proud are scattered and the lowly lifted up. She herself, one of God's 'little ones', was to be God-bearer. Mary, we are told, thought deeply. The poor shepherds in the neighbouring fields perhaps helped her develop a concept of the kind of kingship her Son's was destined to be. Jesus would one day shepherd his people. He was not going to eat with the righteous but with sinners; his disciples would be working people, not rabbis. This perhaps is why Luke includes the story of the shepherds in his narrative, not to provide interesting biographical details about Jesus' early life, but to help us understand the thrust of the good news.

The imagery of shepherds carried meaning for people of Luke's day, as did the setting in Bethlehem. Luke was at pains to emphasize Christ's birth in the place David was born because early Christians saw Christ as true King of the Jews, a shepherd-king like David. The prophets had described God himself as our shepherd. When Jesus called himself the Good Shepherd the image carried immediate impact: God in Jesus guides, protects, cares for his people, and leads them to good pasture. He gave up his own life for his 'flock', and said to Peter, 'Take care of my lambs' (John 21.15). The shepherd's crook still symbolizes leadership in the Church.

Christian love, it seems, is inextricably caught up with shepherding. The idea, however, is more romantic than the reality of looking after people day in and day out. If we are a carer to a sick or elderly relative or a parent of young children, we may know well what it is to feel cut off from normal society in a mundane routine which is full of hardship and far from glorious. Our senses may be all too aware of the everyday reality of struggling humanity; our sacrifice, like Jesus', may go unappreciated.

It is at such moments that we can call to mind the shepherds' sign. The assurance of God's love was simply this: look out for a baby in rags lying in a feeding trough. Like the shepherds, we do not have to look far: vulnerable people are still everywhere about us, still wrapped in different guises, still suffering indignities. And where we find them, we will also meet with instances of charitable support, neighbourly interest, family loyalty, joy amid poverty, and strangers brought in from the cold. What clearer signs do we need that God is still incarnate in the world he loves?

If we are serious about finding God, then we must stop looking 'up' or 'afar' and start looking 'down' and 'nearby' instead, to notice what is in human eyes small, commonplace and insignificant. We will need to acknowledge the poor and ragged, the lonely and awkward. We will need to recognize our own littleness and inadequacies. It may even be helpful to recall the school nativity play, our own or our children's . . . shepherds wearing tea-towels on their heads; angels swathed in tinfoil; a doll bundled unceremoniously into straw; loud stage whispers to a Joseph with stage-fright; and the 'tears and smiles' the baby Jesus knew matched by the tears and smiles of parents and grandparents. Remember how children and adults alike understood that the shepherds' gift of a lamb was received no less graciously than the treasures of the Kings . . . how is it that we have forgotten this simple but important truth?

Jesus must find room in us. It is *our* pride that must be scattered; *our* fullness that must be emptied. It is a human tendency to make more of ourselves than we are, to boast about our achievements, compete for recognition, and defend or conceal our mistakes. Yet none of our cleverness, generosity or charitable efforts can advance the kingdom without God's collaboration; none of our motives are pure. Once we recognize our dependency upon God and stop trying to distance ourselves from our humanity, we are beginning to follow the Good Shepherd.

The learning for us may be to simplify our lives, to de-clutter our living space, to clear our speech of affectation, to give up emotional games, and our attempts to impress or entertain. Finding God may turn out to be the same road we travel to find ourselves, both ordinary and incomparably loved, dark-natured yet shining with God's glory. We might start today to take off some of the wrappings and dare to be just as we are. Humility is not self-deprecation any more than it is self-glorification: it is to see ourselves honestly. God asks us to let go of our sophistication. Mary and Joseph were content to be companion to the ox and ass, grateful for the charity of the sympathetic but hard-pressed innkeeper. There, too, in a more humble stance, the heavenly host will be able to find us. It is through Bethlehem that any spiritual journey must wend its way.

Personal Reflection Time

➢ What would 'peace on earth' consist of for me?

➢ The shepherds were given proofs of God's love for humankind. What signs do I see in my life?

➢ Imagine yourself surrounded by 'a great army of heaven's angels'. Praise God with them.

Prayer

To find God as a baby
Let us go to Bethlehem

To find glory in humility
Let us go to Bethlehem

To find joy amid poverty
Let us go to Bethlehem

To find our peace in simplicity
Let us go to Bethlehem

We remember before God . . .

- Those who sleep rough
- Migrant families
- Childless couples

Activities to Consider

❖ Turn out some of your possessions (or your children's unwanted toys) and offer them to a charity shop or a children's hospice.

❖ Prepare a crib set ready for Christmas.

❖ Contact someone in need of some cheering news or a visit.

3

Within reach

. . . of the elderly

Luke 2.25–35

At that time there was a man named Simeon living in Jerusalem. He was a good, devout man and was waiting for Israel to be saved. The Holy Spirit was with him and had assured him that he would not die before he had seen the Lord's promised Messiah. Led by the Spirit, Simeon went into the Temple. When the parents brought the child Jesus into the Temple to do for him what the Law required, Simeon took the child in his arms and gave thanks to God:

> *'Now, Lord, you have kept your promise,*
> *and you may let your servant go in peace.*
> *With my own eyes I have seen your salvation,*
> *which you have prepared in the presence of all peoples:*
> *A light to reveal your will to the Gentiles*
> *and bring glory to your people Israel.'*

The child's father and mother were amazed at the things Simeon said about him. Simeon blessed them and said to Mary, his mother, 'This child is chosen by God for the destruction and the salvation of many in Israel. He will be a sign from God which many people will speak against and

*so reveal their secret thoughts. And sorrow, like a sharp
sword, will break your own heart.'*

Waiting is not something that most people find easy.
Accompanying my mother to the local shops as a small child
seemed to involve no end of waiting while she queued or
chatted. I remember pulling at my mother's hand and rearran-
ging the sawdust on the butcher's floor with the toe of my
shoes, longing for her to be done. Children of my generation,
it seems, were always being told to stand still and be quiet. I
hated waiting.

Stillness and quiet can be difficult to cope with, even as
adults. We may be plunged into inactivity against our will if
retirement comes too suddenly or if our health fails us. On
retreat we are waiting on God: this, like any other experience
of waiting, may be associated with frustration and the waste
of precious time. Disillusionment can quickly set in if nothing
seems to 'happen'. At the back of our minds there lurks an
anxiety . . . will God come to me?

Old Simeon had every reason to feel impatience and anxiety. He had spent his whole life waiting for a Messiah. He
was aware of his own nation's desperate need for moral and
spiritual renewal, and daily reminders of the Roman army
of occupation made him all too aware of the pagan world
beyond. He longed for the Saviour foretold in ancient prophecy, but he was not fretful, for he had absolute faith that God
would fulfil the promise he had made. More than that, he
believed he would not die until the Saviour had come.

Faith makes waiting a very different kind of experience.
Trusting that the longed-for Christ would certainly come,
however long it took, transformed Simeon's waiting into
joyful anticipation. It freed him to live every moment to the
full in an attitude of humble receptivity. Seeing everything

as demonstrations of the loving providence and presence of God, Simeon, when the moment came, had no difficulty (as we might) in recognizing the Christ-child. His whole life had prepared him to welcome Love into the world.

Waiting was not about emptiness or wasted time, but about making space for Christ and being focused. His was an attitude of thankfulness, and the awareness of every moment's potential for gift. We too can be watchful for God's movement in our world and in our lives right now. Instead of willing God to come to us, we can remember ways in which he has already blessed us with his love and goodness. Learning to recognize God's presence in the ordinary encounters of our day enables us to live fully in the present moment. The presence of God is not to be found in a separate time or place from the one in which we find ourselves.

Far from being a negative experience, waiting was transformative for Simeon: a lifetime of loving attentiveness had produced in him the very qualities of the Saviour he was expecting. God's own Spirit was with him, giving him the kind of insight we read about in this passage. Described as 'good' and 'devout', we observe that he was also spontaneous in his prayer life, likely to burst at any moment into joyful praise of God. At other times he was, like Jesus, unafraid to voice uncomfortable truths, even if it meant warning a new mother that her child would bring her pain as well as happiness. The central drama of Simeon's life was the moment he took the baby Jesus into his arms. God's gift of himself was beyond anything he could have imagined. He saw that the promised Messiah was more than a prophet or king: God himself had become man in order to share our lives and lead us out of darkness.

Jesus, however, was not universally welcomed or recognized. The good news addressed to the wider population of the unclean, diseased and poor, enthralling them with the message that they were forgiven, healed and honoured in God's kingdom, proved radically divisive. Reinstating God's 'little ones' threatened the powerful and proud. Jesus directly challenged the outward piety and hypocrisy of the Pharisees and Jewish authorities. This was perhaps what Simeon meant when he foretold that the child would bring destruction and a disclosing of uncomfortable truths. His mother would one day face the anguish of seeing this controversial Saviour pay the ultimate price of voicing the pain of his people's oppression: he would share it. So what was it about his message that people found unacceptable? Simply this: that God loves us . . . all of us without exception even as we are.

Acceptance is as much a problem for us as it was for the people of Jesus' day. Deep down many of us feel unloved and therefore unloving, rejected and therefore sour. Sometimes our early life has made us so. Perhaps there were no dutiful parents like Mary and Joseph to do the right thing by us, no encouraging adults of Simeon's kind to take us into their arms. Without blessing or praise, we may grow up with very low opinions of ourselves. We too are invited, as Simeon was, to take the baby Jesus into our arms. By accepting God's gift of love, we are, in a sense, also accepting ourselves.

How unlike the Christ-child we become as we grow to adulthood! Babies trust: they have to, for they cannot provide for themselves. Babies have none of the clever conversation, pleasing behaviours or affectations adopted by adults to keep other people from seeing the real person beneath. They can only express their simple needs and just 'be'. No wonder Jesus said that to enter the kingdom of God we must become like children again. He was not recommending regressive behaviour, just reminding us to allow our heavenly Father to take care of us, and to content ourselves with being who we are without dissemblance. Like Simeon in his prophecy, babies make no attempt to disguise the truth or to make it more palatable. Jesus, even as an adult, did not hide his feelings. 'You have eyes – can't you see?' (Mark 8.18) he said bluntly to those who failed to recognize God at work in their lives.

Simeon saw only too clearly. Thirty years later his prophecy was to be literally played out when Jesus, full of righteous anger, entered the exclusive temple precincts to drive out traders and money-changers. As Jesus pointed out, the peace he gives is not freedom from trouble, but the peace of mind that comes from living justly and utterly truthfully, with all the social costs and personal sacrifices that congruence and integrity inevitably involve. The light of Christ can indeed be a glaring beam revealing aspects of ourselves that we as individuals and as a society would rather leave undetected.

What will this waiting time of retreat be like for us? The light of Christ's truth discloses the truer picture: that we are unique, flawed but precious, and unconditionally loved. This is the way Christ sees us. Known and forgiven, released from the desperate need to disguise our vulnerabilities, our thoughts can be revealed without fear that we will be rejected or shamed. We will find ourselves, like Simeon, more available to other people, more likely to recognize Christ's presence in the stranger, and both parties in the encounter will find it a source of blessing.

The Church still honours the memory of this prophet who bravely heralded Christ's long-awaited presence to a needy world. The Presentation of the Lord, or by its older name Candlemas, is celebrated 40 days after Christmas when church candles are blessed for use during the year and when Christ is greeted as Light of the nations. In the prayer of the Church, the Song of Simeon, known by its opening words in Latin, the Nunc Dimittis, is recited as day draws to its close. The world is still in need of light, but God's people can, as Simeon did, face life – and death – in perfect trust. Our Saviour is come to us.

Personal Reflection Time

➢ Light a candle. What is it that your 'eyes have seen' today to remind you of God's love?

➢ Thank God for anyone you have met or may encounter today. Recognize the light they shed.

➢ Imagine taking the baby Jesus into your arms from his mother Mary. What is he like?

Prayer

How you have loved me
Open my eyes to see

How you have guided me
Open my eyes to see

How you have provided
Open my eyes to see

How you have protected
Open my eyes to see

You reveal your love for me
Open my eyes to see

This moment is your gift
Open my eyes to see

We remember in prayer . . .

- Those waiting to be born

- Those preparing to die

- Those learning to be parents

Activities to Consider

❖ Find a photograph of yourself as a baby. What do you see?

❖ Take the opportunity to speak to someone you would not normally approach.

❖ Say or do something supportive for any young parents you know.

4

Within reach

...of the parent

Luke 2.41–52

Every year the parents of Jesus went to Jerusalem for the Passover Festival. When Jesus was twelve years old, they went to the festival as usual. When the festival was over, they started back home, but the boy Jesus stayed in Jerusalem. His parents did not know this; they thought that he was with the group, so they travelled a whole day and then started looking for him among their relatives and friends. They did not find him, so they went back to Jerusalem looking for him. On the third day they found him in the Temple, sitting with the Jewish teachers, listening to them and asking questions. All who heard him were amazed at his intelligent answers. His parents were astonished when they saw him, and his mother said to him, 'My son, why have you done this to us? Your father and I have been terribly worried trying to find you.'

He answered them, 'Why did you have to look for me? Didn't you know that I had to be in my Father's house?' But they did not understand his answer.

So Jesus went back with them to Nazareth, where he was obedient to them. His mother treasured all these things in her heart. Jesus grew both in body and in wisdom, gaining favour with God and men.

One seaside holiday my family will never forget was when, as a child, I became separated from my parents in the crowds. Panicking at the realization that I was lost, I ran. Heading away from where they were, I pushed my way towards Yarmouth Pier, knowing that we had a family booking for the Lonnie Donegan concert that evening. It never occurred to me that they would cancel all their plans once they realized I was lost; it never occurred to them that I would move from the spot they last saw me. Our eventual reunion was a tearful one, full of mutual recrimination as well as relief.

The story of Jesus getting lost must have been written down a very long time after the event took place, yet there is something so familiar about its conflicting perceptions of what went wrong and the panic expressed as anger that lends an air of authenticity to this cameo of his early earthly life. Mary and Joseph's mood, mellowed by the holiday festivities in Jerusalem, turned to anger and fear when Jesus appeared to be behaving irresponsibly. The boy, like most pre-teens, was no doubt absorbed in his own developing interests and just lost sense of time.

He seemed hurt that those closest to him had so little understanding of him that they would look for him every-where but where he was most likely to be. They must have noticed how deep an impression this new experience of temple worship had made upon him during the Passover, and observed his daily reluctance to leave the temple courts. Yet his parents had different ideas about where home was and what constituted being lost. For Mary and Joseph, home was in the family circle back in Nazareth. They considered him to be 'lost' when he failed to be in the place they wanted him to be – that is, with their neighbours and friends. Jesus, on the other hand, at home in the temple, could not conceive how anyone could be considered lost in the presence of God.

Our own spiritual journey may take us along a similar road to Mary's and Joseph's whenever we take it for granted that Jesus is going along with everything we are doing and thinking. There comes a point in our lives when we sense his absence. Like them, we may regard Jesus as 'lost' and start to search frantically, blaming God, and defensive about our own part. Perhaps we have wanted Jesus to be in the company *we* want to be in and heading in the direction *we* determine for ourselves.

Perhaps we are keen to keep him, like all good children, 'seen and not heard'. Jesus, on the other hand, challenges our perception that he has ever been lost to us. He has always been right where we might expect to find him – if we really knew what he was like, that is – in places of worship, among the poor and needy, mingling with the crowd of strangers and travellers. We should know well enough.

Maybe it is easier for us to feel that he is 'naughty' or 'lost' than to be with him in the places we know he regards as home. Often the place we steadfastly refuse to accept that Jesus regards as home is within ourselves, despite Jesus' assurances. As he said on the night before his death, 'Whoever loves me will obey my teaching. My Father will love him, and my Father and I will come to him and live with him' (John 14.23). We become the temple of God's Holy Spirit, the place where Jesus feels at home, when we follow what we know to be right.

What is it that makes us frantically search everywhere but where we know him to be? It begs a question about our commitment to the things most important to Jesus: too often we want him to be with us where *we* want to go rather than for us to be with him on the margins where *he* needs to stay. It exposes our reluctance to explore issues that are difficult and personally challenging, unlike the boy Jesus who courageously entered debate with Jewish teachers. Home for us so often means a comfort zone where we can build religious faith into a cosy corner. Home for Jesus was never about somewhere to rest his head.

Our unwillingness to accept what we know Jesus is like may prompt us to consider how accepting we are of people generally. It is easier for us to feel that other people are 'lost' than to acknowledge that we are being controlling, taking them for granted, or failing to understand and respect their growth and autonomy. It is especially easy to do it with children. Our loved ones are people in their own right and not extensions of ourselves. Next time we are about to say, 'Why have you done this to us?' it might be wise to consider how we have treated them.

The three days of anxiety – or perhaps that is how long it seemed – must have been a very dark time for Jesus' parents. The three days are reminiscent of the three days following the crucifixion when Mary experienced losing her son again. This time she shared the anguish with disciples like Cleopas and his wife. They set off in a dejected mood to Emmaus, believing that they had lost Jesus for ever. The story is a mirror image of 30 years previously, when Mary and Joseph set off believing that Jesus was in their company while all along they had left him behind in Jerusalem; Cleopas and his wife believed they had left Jesus behind them in Jerusalem, only to find that he was in their company all along. Each couple found him after a period of three days. 'Stay with us,' they said to Jesus, and he did, just as he had obediently accompanied his parents to Nazareth. In both stories, the couples retrace their steps and go back to Jerusalem at great speed. Both find Jesus and are changed in the process of discovering him in a new way: Mary 'treasured . . . in her heart' the sight of him among the wise and learned; Cleopas and his wife were 'burning' inside as he explained the deep wisdom of scripture to them.

We too must go back to the places where we know deep down that we will find Jesus. We must retrace our steps to the centre of worship; back to the heart of things, especially to the heart of ourselves; back to a more humble stance where we ask questions and listen to the wisdom of others; back to the re-reading of scripture through which Jesus can help us to understand who he really is; back to the breaking of bread where our eyes can be opened and we can recognize him afresh.

The lost-child story is one with which we all connect: so often we were the ones who were lost as children. That terrifying realization of separation is a feeling some of us take into adulthood, ever the 'abandoned child', the child accused of being naughty for reasons we did not always understand. With God's help, we can find the lost child within ourselves and take him or her home. Voicing our needs is a good start. Perhaps, like Jesus, there is a particular place where *we* need to be rather than always having to follow the crowd when it heads off without checking to see whether we are ready or want to come. Perhaps, like him, there are people *we* need to talk to who can help us find answers that satisfy. Perhaps, like him, the time has come for *us* to astonish other people by doing something that reveals our individuality and potential.

Jesus' description as 'obedient' implies a blind compliance with other people's wishes. Yet, for him, growing in favour of God came before growing in popularity with other people. The root of the word 'obey' means to 'listen'. This story demonstrates that for Jesus, obedience was an attitude of listening in order to understand the will of his Father. Jesus continues to ask and answer questions as he sits in the temple of our hearts, helping us to hear and understand what God is saying to us. We may discover that God's dream for us is not so very different from the dream we have for ourselves.

Personal Reflection Time

➢ Which memories of youth can I treasure in my heart?

➢ Who are the wisdom figures in my life, and what questions do I want to ask them?

➢ Where do I feel most at home? What does that tell me about who I am?

Prayer

> Lord Jesus,
>
> Your quiet company
> **I treasure in my heart**
>
> Your patient listening
> **I treasure in my heart**
>
> Your searching questions
> **I treasure in my heart**
>
> Your will above mine
> **I treasure in my heart**

We remember in prayer . . .

- Missing children
- Youth workers
- Foster carers

Activities to Consider

❖ Find a photograph of yourself when you were about 12. What were you like?

❖ If you still have one, ask an older relative what memories they treasure of the things you did or said as a child.

❖ In your next conversation, practise listening instead of talking, especially if you are with children.

5

Within reach

. . . of the young

John 1.35-42

The next day John was standing there again with two of his disciples, when he saw Jesus walking by. 'There is the Lamb of God!' he said.

The two disciples heard him say this and went with Jesus. Jesus turned, saw them following him, and asked, 'What are you looking for?'

They answered, 'Where do you live, Rabbi?' (This word means 'Teacher'.)

'Come and see,' he answered. (It was then about four o'clock in the afternoon.) So they went with him and saw where he lived, and spent the rest of that day with him.

One of them was Andrew, Simon Peter's brother. At once he found his brother Simon and told him, 'We have found the Messiah.' (This word means 'Christ'.) Then he took Simon to Jesus.

Jesus looked at him and said, 'Your name is Simon son of John, but you will be called Cephas.' (This is the same as Peter and means 'a rock'.)

Jesus is still walking by, though we do not always notice. John the Baptist's disciples may not have noticed either, had their master not spotted the unlikely looking working man and cried out, 'There is the Lamb of God!' He knew that God's Anointed would not be carrying a sword or wearing a crown, that he was destined to sacrifice his own life like a lamb to the slaughter. That was something the young men would take a long while to understand.

'What are you looking for?' is the question Jesus asked them and one that he asks us too. What *are* we looking for? Someone powerful who will take control of our world and make it a safer place in which to live? A Superman who will champion us in every personal battle? The first thing we learn in Jesus' company is that he does not rescue us from our reality – he enters it.

'What do you ask of us?' was the question put to me during the ceremony of initiation to the religious life. To learn your way of life and follow Christ crucified began the expected answer, though lurking in the corners of my heart were other motivations. The hope of achieving special intimacy with God was one of them, and I hoped to do that by becoming a different person. Community life, however, with all its ups and downs, merely revealed more of that 'not-so-good' self I was trying to evade. I found that the path to God is also the path of self-knowledge. Eventually the day came when I could pray to become more and more the person God made me.

Self-acceptance requires the right environment. Jesus' invitation to John's disciples on that significant day in Capernaum carried no conditions. He required nothing of them, not even any commitment to follow his teachings, and did not begin their relationship by stipulating what needed changing. Welcoming them unconditionally just as they were, the very power of the presence of Jesus worked a transformation.

John the Baptist understood his role in this. Though he had

every reason to keep his young disciples at his own side, he let them continue their personal search for fulfilment and pointed them in the right direction. We too need sometimes to let go for the sake of another's growth. How influential we can be in pointing people to the right things . . . or the wrong things. Peter, the Rock on whom Christ founded his Church, found Jesus only because his brother loved him enough to arrange the meeting.

The story of the two disciples took a rather surprising turn when they simply went home with Jesus. At this discovery of the Messiah, the reader might expect a crowd to gather, a great announcement to be made, or a miracle to mark the event. Instead, Jesus invited the disciples to see where he lived and they simply spent the rest of the day with him. A historic moment turned out to be a rather homely one. Jesus does not invite us to strenuous feats of spiritual endurance or asceticism either. We are not all John the Baptists, living on locusts and wild honey, nor does Jesus measure commitment by weight of words or the length of our prayer times. Quantity is not the criterion: relationship is. As the prophet Micah reminded us, all that is required of us is to be fair and kind to other people and to walk humbly with our God. Walking humbly with Jesus is exactly what the disciples did.

Relationship-building is at the heart of our spiritual life as well as our social, working and family life. Religion cannot remain a personal hobby to occupy our spare time. Getting to know Jesus takes time, like any relationship, and we need to work at it. Learning to relate is fundamental to our happiness. If we can only accept Jesus' challenges and rebukes, valuable lessons from our humble walking with God may well transform our other relationships too. We may realize how little attention we really give to others, talking but not really listening, looking but not really noticing. John the Baptist taught his disciples to see beyond themselves: 'There is the Lamb of God!' At the root of relationship is time spent together that really *sees* and *hears* the other.

Jesus perhaps is asking us to sit with him for a while. A contemplative stance is very hard for modern Western people who are programmed to 24/7 activity. 'Being' requires practice and the right conditions: somewhere away from distractions, a comfortable and private place where we can feel at home with Jesus and ourselves. No effort to make conversation is required of us: words are not necessary at all. Jesus in this passage is the host and it is up to him to entertain his guests appropriately. Jesus, we are told, just looked at Peter. We need to sit still long enough to let that happen to us.

'Being' sometimes has to be planned. Most people choose the quiet of early morning, but there can be graced moments that arise unexpectedly – as they did for Andrew and his companion. For them it came in the middle of the afternoon. No doubt they had other plans, but they were spontaneous enough to leave everything and to follow Jesus. We too need to be detached enough to respond to God's invitations. Even a couple of moments on a bus can be enough time to expand our awareness of the presence of Jesus. Being able to say with Andrew, 'We have found the Messiah' is to be assured that he is always passing by.

Spending our day – every day – in the company of Jesus has a transforming effect. It usually leads to a change of allegiance. The disciples stopped following John and followed Jesus instead. It was not that there was anything wrong with following John the Baptist – on the contrary, he had prepared them for this time – but their ultimate vocation was to be Jesus' disciples. For us, too, there may be a moving on, whether that involves some slight adjustment to our routine or a radical redirection when we recognize what our personal calling really is. We may find that we begin to bear a family likeness to our new master. Andrew soon found himself saying and doing what Jesus did when he invited his brother to 'come and see'.

For Simon, being with Jesus meant not just a change of occupation, but a change of name. Jesus saw not Simon, the fisherman's son, but the Rock. John the Baptist had that gift: he saw not his cousin, the carpenter's son, but the Lamb of God. When Jesus looks at us, he sees not the person we and others know, but the essence of our self, the goodness, strength and potential we scarcely acknowledge ourselves. When we look at other people, even very familiar people, perhaps we might start to perceive with the loving eyes of Jesus a person we may not have recognized before. People have a tendency to live up to expectations.

It can nevertheless be unnerving to be looked at penetratingly. Everyone fears the exposure of shames and weaknesses lurking under the persona we present to a critical world. Jesus sees beyond even these underlying aspects to the deepest level where he himself can be at home. When we ask Jesus, 'Where do you live, Rabbi?', Jesus takes us into our hidden selves and shows us this very surprising place where he feels quite comfortable. There is a strong sense of kinship throughout this passage: we read of brothers, cousins and sons. When Jesus takes us home, it is not to view the decor, but to be part of his family.

John the Baptist really was related to Jesus, but it took years for John to recognize Jesus as God's Anointed. Even before he encountered Jesus, he simply lived his life under God's searching, loving gaze. The gaze of God sees through to the essential person, and before long the peripherals of life must have seemed irrelevant to John too. Wearing a camel-skin, he no longer dressed to impress anyone; eating from the wild, he stopped living to please himself. There were no miraculous feats. Without fear or favour he simply told home truths, sometimes very challenging ones. People were drawn to him nevertheless. His message to them was to repent – to turn round their lives and prepare for the day when Jesus would walk by. Today may be that very day for us.

Personal Reflection Time

➢ How would I reply to Jesus' question, 'What are you looking for?'

➢ At four o'clock today, accept Jesus' invitation to go home with him. Let your imagination take you there.

➢ Jesus looked at Peter and gave him a name that summed him up as a person. Look at yourself: what positive qualities can you see?

Prayer

Look at me
Lamb of God

Love me as I am
Lamb of God

See to the heart of me
Lamb of God

Help me recognize myself
Lamb of God

Take me home to who I am
Lamb of God

We thank God for . . .

- Those who have told us home-truths

- Those who have helped us move on

- Those who have recognized our potential

Activities to Consider

❖ Invite someone to spend a day with you.

❖ Find out the meaning of your own name, and perhaps those of people close to you.

❖ Contact your brother, sister or a friend you have not spoken to for a while to catch up on each other's news.

6

Within reach

. . . of the crowd

Mark 1.45; 5.17; 5.24; 6.31; 6.54–6; 9.15; 10.13

*Jesus could not go into a town publicly. Instead, he stayed
out in lonely places, and people came to him from everywhere . . .*

. . . they asked Jesus to leave their territory . . .

*So many people were going along with Jesus that they
were crowding him from every side . . .*

*There were so many people coming and going that Jesus
and his disciples didn't even have time to eat . . .*

*As they left the boat, people recognized Jesus at once. So
they ran throughout the whole region; and wherever they
heard he was, they brought to him sick people lying on their
mats. And everywhere Jesus went, to villages, towns, or
farms, people would take those who were ill to the market
places and beg him to let them at least touch the edge of his
cloak; and all who touched it were made well . . .*

When the people saw Jesus, they . . . ran to him . . .

*. . . people brought children to Jesus for him to place his
hands on them . . .*

People like me who grew up in the era of Beatle-mania have

some idea of how a movement can mushroom overnight. I remember news coverage of the screaming fans who accompanied the Beatles' every journey without thought of propriety or safety. My best friend excited much envy among us by picking what she claimed to be a leaf from the hedge in front of Paul McCartney's family home. It was revered as a relic. Sometimes our parents laughed; occasionally, I think, they panicked.

Jesus' appeal was not confined to teenagers, nor was it hysteria, yet the early chapters of Mark's Gospel paint a picture of Galilean society thrown into disarray by the excitement he was creating. Normally prudent people were behaving with an impetuosity never seen before, leaving their homes and jobs late into the day without a thought for what they might eat or where they could sleep. This was an extravagant response to something that had never happened before and that might never happen again. People were behaving as though life as they had known it had ended and a new time had begun. The kingdom of God had arrived. A sense of immediacy and of limitless possibility had broken into their old world of disease, death, oppression and the daily grind to survive, and it was electrifying. People were running, pleading, begging. Nothing else mattered. Jesus was near. Who needed to eat?

No one at this stage seemed to have reached any conclusions as to Jesus' true identity: all they knew was that they felt an irresistible pull towards this ordinary-looking man. This was something more than celebrity-fever, more than a frenzied attempt to cash in on free cures, more than a bit of sensationalism to liven up their dull existence. What was it they wanted? To touch him, mostly . . . the mere brush of his clothes as he passed; and especially for him to lay his hands on their children and sick relatives. It was something to do with the power of 'presence'. The disciples' healing powers were not enough, even though we are told that they were able to exorcize demons and anoint sick people. When Jesus appeared on the scene, people were overcome with emotion and ran to him instead. The person of Jesus was the object of their desire much more than any favours he might bestow.

These moving Gospel accounts suggest that, however urgent the medical needs of those lakeside communities, what people wanted from Jesus was the healing that comes with empathy, forgiveness, acceptance and a sense of belonging. It is interesting to see how the sick and vulnerable were prioritized by the crowd. It was as if people understood instinctively what Jesus stood for, that he had come to God's little ones, the least in the kingdom of this world. It was good news indeed that at last someone acknowledged their pain.

More than that, Jesus was bringing God into the here-and-now. God is so unutterably holy that Jews dared not even refer to him by name. The experience of being with Jesus must have *felt* like being in the presence of a holiness that cannot be described. He was a creative and re-creative energy. There was an indefinable quality of 'God-with-us' about Jesus, even before he made his controversial claim to be one with the Father. Whenever you were with him, that empty, lonely and sometimes frightening sense of separation that everyone experiences from time to time, whether they acknowledge it or not, simply melted away.

Not everyone was thrilled. The authorities were evidently anxious: they did not want to provoke the Roman occupying forces, always nervous about potential rebellion, into any premature reaction. Then there were the family and friends of Jesus, who seemed offended at his sudden cult-status and blamed him for colluding with public mania. Even Jesus' disciples were sometimes terrified at the extremes of Jesus' behaviour. The story of Jesus walking on water is very telling:

if he gained a reputation for challenging the laws of nature, he probably pushed quite a few other boundaries first.

It is difficult to ascertain the extent to which Jesus welcomed fame. There are plenty of Gospel references to him silencing those who had been cured or who guessed his true identity. Equally, we see him making inflammatory statements and sending out disciples two-by-two to prepare villages for his arrival. What seems clear is that he did not encourage sensationalism: the healing miracles were wrested from his compassionate nature almost as by-products of his main purpose, which was to enlighten the people to a greater understanding of their own faith in a God who is intimately and compassionately involved in everyday human lives.

The Galilean townsfolk could not wander about indefinitely in the wake of Jesus. At some point they had to resume their lives. He told the demoniac to go home, and showed concern for the physical well-being of the 5,000 he fed. We cannot live on a permanent spiritual 'high' any more than they could. The kingdom of God, as Jesus tried to explain, does not entail physical removal to another sphere; rather, it is the living out of the familiar sphere with a different outlook. The mundane is not to be shunned, but transformed. It is not so much about enduring this life in the hope of a heavenly reward as about quality of living, starting right now.

Life-to-the-full, which may have been part of what Jesus was describing as the kingdom of God, is amply sketched even in these few short sentences scattered about in Mark's early chapters. The mere news of Jesus' arrival was enough to end discrimination as the sick and vulnerable were gently pushed into prominence. Family issues like mental illness and epilepsy, once shamefully concealed behind closed doors, were brought into the open as sufferers were laid out in the market-places. Pressing forward to touch Jesus, people found that they were touched by one another in the amiable jostling of the crowd. Weather and politics were replaced by talk of God as neighbours started to engage with one another at a deeper level. People discovered a liberating sense of mobility and freedom as they traversed the hills, sharing provisions and passing on news of Jesus. The holiness of everyday relationships was like the oil of healing administered by the disciples. No one seemed tired any more, or hungry: a new energy infused people as they ran and walked. Joy, that rare commodity, had returned. No wonder Jesus could say that the kingdom was at hand: he was not giving advance notice so much as watching it unfold before his eyes.

Spontaneity is not the same as impetuosity. Jesus discouraged the rich young ruler from following him as a spur-of-the-moment decision, and stressed the practical implications of discipleship. He also held firm opinions about our responsibility to spouses, children and elderly relatives. He did, however, encourage a greater detachment from things, a simpler way of life, and a more trusting outlook. For Jesus, 'now' was the most important moment: '. . . leave your gift there in front of the altar, go at once and make peace with your brother' (Matthew 5.24). We see that same immediacy in the crowds who followed Jesus. For them, living in the present moment meant finding a quality of life that made what went before seem like mere existence.

Yet so often we choose existence over Life. We are like the authorities who could not countenance change: they would rather be half-dead than lose control of where life was leading. Living fully in the present moment demands that we let go of our self-absorption, schedules and preoccupations and start to be fully 'present' to other people. If we have young children, we may need to take an interest in what they want to tell us and to play with them more. If our children and sick friends are to experience the reassurance of hands placed upon them, then it is going to have to be *our* hands.

It is not easy to live in the 'now'. We quickly slip into worrying about tomorrow or reliving the things that happened yesterday. The moment passes and we miss opportunities for friendship, vistas from the window, the sounds of birds, and the smells of cooking. Yet it is in the simple experiences of this very day, especially in the people we encounter, that we find Jesus among us. As the Psalmist tells us, 'Listen *today* to what he says . . .' (Psalm 95.7).

Personal Reflection Time

➢ Quietly experience this present moment. Notice the sensations of your own body as well as everything that is going on around you.

➢ Lie down. Imagine you are one of the sick lying in a market-place waiting for Jesus to walk by. Let his shadow slowly pass over you. What are you feeling?

➢ What changes do I want to make to the way I engage with people?

Prayer

> On our children
> **Lay your hands**
>
> On our sick
> **Lay your hands**
>
> On my loved ones
> **Lay your hands**

> On this world
> **Lay your hands**
>
> On me, Lord Jesus
> **Lay your hands**

We remember before God . . .

- The vulnerable
- The impressionable
- The untouchable

Activities to Consider

❖ Rediscover the power of touch: for example, take the hand of a sick friend or an elderly person if you feel it would be appropriate and not invasive.

❖ Spend a relaxing few minutes massaging your own hands or feet with some fragrant oil or cream.

❖ Empty your handbag or briefcase . . . how much of this stuff do you really need to keep in it?

7

Within reach

. . . of the paralysed

Mark 2.1–12

A few days later Jesus went back to Capernaum, and the news spread that he was at home. So many people came together that there was no room left, not even out in front of the door. Jesus was preaching the message to them when four men arrived, carrying a paralysed man to Jesus. Because of the crowd, however, they could not get the man to him. So they made a hole in the roof right above the place where Jesus was. When they had made an opening, they let the man down, lying on his mat. Seeing how much faith they had, Jesus said to the paralysed man, 'My son, your sins are forgiven.'

Some teachers of the Law who were sitting there thought to themselves, 'How does he dare to talk like this? This is blasphemy! God is the only one who can forgive sins!'

At once Jesus knew what they were thinking, so he said to them, 'Why do you think such things? Is it easier to say to this paralysed man, "Your sins are forgiven", or to say, "Get up, pick up your mat, and walk"? I will prove to you, then, that the Son of Man has authority on earth to forgive sins.' So he said to the paralysed man, 'I tell you, get up, pick up your mat, and go home!'

While they all watched, the man got up, picked up his mat, and hurried away. They were all completely amazed and praised God, saying, 'We have never seen anything like this!'

It is frustrating to telephone for a medical appointment only to find the receptionist protective of the doctor's diary. The idea of bypassing the secretary and queue of patients by tunnelling directly into the doctor's surgery seems more like material for alternative comedy than for a Gospel narrative. Yet that is more or less what happened when the friends of the paralysed man found that the crowds were too dense for them to find a way through to Jesus the Healer. On this day in Capernaum, which he seems to have made his home-base, the house was enclosed by a solid wall of devoted followers, sensation-seekers and critics. There was no hope of getting through.

It is a shame that, after all these centuries of reflecting on the gospel message, we continue to restrict access to Jesus. Church attendance is still often beyond the reach of people with limited mobility, and a welcome may be restricted to those who conform to a particular social profile. In spite of Jesus' clear statement, 'I have not come to call respectable people, but outcasts' (Mark 2.17), it is also the enduring opinion of many churchgoers that their church *is* for respectable people, and only an inner circle of respectable people at that.

Somehow the four men with the stretcher knew enough about Jesus to feel confident that he would not object to this unorthodox mode of entry. Perhaps they realized that breaking through things was what Jesus himself did all the time. 'Teacher,' said the Pharisees on one occasion, 'we know that you tell the truth, without worrying about what people think. You pay no attention to a man's status . . .' (Mark 12.14). Jesus saw beyond appearance, physical fitness, gender and rank to engage with the person beneath. He was not obsequious when he addressed high-ranking Jewish or Roman officials; he was equally at ease touching lepers. Scandalously for a Jewish man of his time, he conversed with females to whom he was not related, like the woman at the well, and encouraged Mary of Bethany to sit at his feet as though she were engaging in the exclusively male pursuit of theological study.

The hole in the roof was nothing compared with the hole Jesus was punching through traditions that had grown up around the Law. The 'unclean' were not just people of different faiths like the Romans, it was a bracket that had come to include many ordinary Jewish people too. It was popular belief that physical infirmity was punishment for sin. The paralysed man seemed to think so too. By 'forgiving him', Jesus was, in effect, rejecting a discriminatory belief system and demonstrating the all-inclusiveness of God's love. When the paralysed man got up at Jesus' command, it was a breathtaking validation of Jesus' claim to act and teach with authority.

Before we cheer, it is well to remember how we erect barriers of our own. We may find ourselves stacking up between ourselves and God a barricade of guilt and shame, fear of being changed, and the comfort zones and grudges that make us feel secure. The biggest obstacle is our need for forgiveness, but we make it into a reason for avoiding God rather than an urgent case for seeking him. Our self-critic wags a Pharisaic finger and tells us we are too bad for God to love us. Such formidable defences prevent us getting close to other people too. Important though it is to respect boundaries in relationships, it is not good to put unnecessary obstacles in the way of trust and mutual understanding.

Illness is not a punishment for sin, but there is a link between certain kinds of ill-health and stress. Guilt and old sources of shame can be crippling, even paralysing, in terms of our mental and emotional well-being. They may be at the root of the anxiety that makes us susceptible to disease or likely to adopt unhealthy lifestyles. A sense of unworthiness or fear of exposure can keep us from enjoying new experiences, from facing life with confidence, and from changing or growing. They can spoil our relationships with other people by making us passive-aggressive or judgemental. Whether we are actually guilty of wrong-doing or just feel a sense of shame about who we are, to hear a commanding voice telling us that we are forgiven would indeed be freeing and healing. For us to extend that forgiveness to others might be more freeing and healing still.

Seeking forgiveness is not a matter of clearing our consciences in order to walk away from the uncomfortable memory of things we have done wrong. Sin is never a purely personal matter. To be whole and happy people we must recognize our moral responsibilities. We are, whether we like it or not, in relationship with everybody else. Restoring right relationships is at the root of healing, for us and for the world, for forgiveness is inseparable from reconciliation. It may involve putting things right, or apologizing, or giving up what does not belong to us. We may have to offer forgiveness, like Jesus did, before the offending person has even asked for it. The righting of wrong and the healing power of forgiveness involve some kind of costly action on our part, even if it is just to swallow our pride and initiate a conversation. Perhaps we stand round like Pharisees, reprimanding Jesus for forgiving someone so easily, when what we are actually saying is that *we* do not want to forgive.

When the critics of Jesus accused him of treating sin as a light matter, they were perhaps unaware of the implications of the paralysed man's miraculous return to health. He had previously relied on constant help from relatives and friends and on money from begging. Now he had to resume responsibility for himself. That would have been, and still is, no easy matter. For us too, the prospect of feeling better after a long period of debilitation may not outweigh the fear and challenge of having to be more independent. Helplessness can become a familiar friend. We may reject an answered prayer for mercy and forgiveness when we cannot face the life changes that it involves. Not everyone wants to be healed or freed.

The paralysed man also faced exposure. He found himself the focus of a controversy between Jesus and his enemies. We too invite comment, scorn, criticism or even disbelief when we change in any way, even for the better. We open ourselves to ridicule. This is where friends and supporters come in. It was not the faith of the paralysed man that drew the compassion of Jesus, but the faith of those who had supported him against the odds. We can imagine them receiving loud complaints as they scattered those assembled in the room below with dusty debris. Maybe the faith that Jesus praised was not their bold initiative, but the commitment they had made to see their friend through the period of rehabilitation that followed.

Perhaps there has been someone in your life who took on this role, by remembering you in prayer or sitting up late to hear your anxieties. Perhaps it is only now that you recognize the need for support in your spiritual life or the help you may be in a position to offer to another. It may be a case of asking someone else to move out of the way to let you through to a more direct and personal experience of Jesus. In effecting changes in our lives, especially when it involves making amends or restoring broken relationships, we all need encouragement and understanding.

Whatever misgivings the healed man may have had, and whatever problems Jesus had introduced for the teachers of the Law in his audience, other onlookers were full of gratitude. As far as they were concerned, authority to speak for God had slipped from the teachers of the Law to Jesus. God's 'little ones' had broken through to where healing and forgiveness could be had for free, and it was a matter for rejoicing. Yet it earned Jesus the implacable hostility of scribes and Pharisees whose power and status depended on keeping things the way they were. For Jesus, the price of forgiving would be his own life.

Personal Reflection Time

➤ Which memories 'paralyse' me? Dare I carry them to Jesus?

➤ What forgiveness do I ask or am I ready to extend?

➤ What obstacles lie in the way of a closer relationship with Jesus? Whose help or encouragement do I need to overcome them?

Prayer

When there is no room for frailty
Jesus, forgive me

When there is no room for toleration
Jesus, forgive me

When there is no room for compassion
Jesus, forgive me

When there is no room for you
Jesus, forgive me

We remember before God . . .

- People with disabilities

- Paramedics and carers

- The work of charities

Activities to Consider

❖ Make an opening in your diary for someone who needs it. It may be you.

❖ If you have your own car, offer a lift to someone with mobility issues who may need to go shopping, to church or attend an appointment.

❖ Do something creative to make your home/church/workplace a more welcoming environment.

8

Within reach

. . . of the small

Luke 19.1–10

*Jesus went on into Jericho and was passing through. There
was a chief tax collector there named Zacchaeus, who was
rich. He was trying to see who Jesus was, but he was a little
man and could not see Jesus because of the crowd. So he ran
ahead of the crowd and climbed a sycomore tree to see Jesus,
who was going to pass that way. When Jesus came to that
place, he looked up and said to Zacchaeus, 'Hurry down,
Zacchaeus, because I must stay in your house today.'*

*Zacchaeus hurried down and welcomed him with great
joy. All the people who saw it started grumbling, 'This man
has gone as a guest to the home of a sinner!'*

*Zacchaeus stood up and said to the Lord, 'Listen, sir!
I will give half my belongings to the poor, and if I have
cheated anyone, I will pay him back four times as much.'*

*Jesus said to him, 'Salvation has come to this house today,
for this man, also, is a descendant of Abraham. The Son of
Man came to seek and to save the lost.'*

People of my age loved to play 'cowboys and indians' when
we were children. Back then, there seemed no question about

which ones were the 'goodies' and which the 'baddies', though nowadays native Americans are regarded as heroes for defending their ancestral territories. In these politically more correct times, we may feel we have grown out of splitting people into 'camps'. Sadly, each generation finds its own way of assigning unofficial roles that disguise the real people beneath. Names like 'hoodie' or 'yuppie' become, in time, dictionary definitions.

Gospel writers reflected the views of their own society by bracketing people together in the same way: scribes, Pharisees, tax collectors and Romans are clearly labelled 'baddies', in spite of some notable exceptions. The tax collector in first-century Palestine was doubly denigrated since he was presumed to be collaborating with the occupying Roman forces as well as fleecing his own people. Zacchaeus, a chief tax collector, seemed unquestionably a 'sinner'.

For anyone familiar with popular psychology, the story of Zacchaeus is reminiscent of the 'Drama Triangle' whereby people in a group situation take up one of three roles: Victim, Persecutor or Rescuer. Though they may switch places, people become locked into the triangle. You may recognize the 'Drama Triangle' in your own relationships. Jesus demonstrates that we do not have to fall into a scripted part in someone else's drama. Sinful Zacchaeus was already cast in the role of 'Persecutor' before the story begins. The crowd certainly regarded themselves as his 'Victims'. They looked to Jesus as 'Rescuer' and expected him to condemn Zacchaeus. Jesus, however, declined to be a crowd-pleaser. Able to 'look above' the prejudice, literally in this case as he glanced up at the tree to notice Zacchaeus, he did not call him down with a view to haranguing him.

Generations of Sunday School children have watched Zacchaeus in their imagination climbing shamefacedly down from the tree. They will have associated it with their own humiliation when, caught hiding, they were suddenly exposed to the anger of adults. We all know that moment of shame as hidden sins are brought into the light of day. Zacchaeus, small of stature, seems suddenly vulnerable in this story. As we hear the muttering of the crowd, rigid and blaming, we find that the crowd and Zacchaeus have switched roles: the crowd have become 'Persecutor' and Zacchaeus the 'Victim'.

Still Jesus resisted being pushed into a set role. He was evidently not motivated by the need to fall in with popular opinion nor programmed to rescue the underdog, nor was self-preservation his first instinct. Jesus simply did not seem to care what people thought about him: if he went along with anything, it was always with whatever was 'right' and with whatever was authentic. Calling Zacchaeus down from the tree exposed the little man to the attention of an angry crowd, but kindness, as far as Jesus was concerned, was not about avoiding issues. He took no one's side: he neither reprimanded nor rescued Zacchaeus. To everyone's astonishment, he simply stepped 'outside the triangle' and asked Zacchaeus' help: 'I must stay in your house today.'

The crowd, outraged, turned its finger-wagging instead towards Jesus: 'This man has gone as a guest to the home of a sinner!' It looks as if Zacchaeus was going to switch roles with Jesus: taking on the role of 'Rescuer', Zacchaeus offered to reimburse anyone who felt cheated. Jesus, however, did not need rescuing. He was not going to be blocked from making choices by self-pity or dejection. 'Poor me' is not one of the recorded sayings of Jesus. He declined the role of 'Victim' just as he refused to be 'Persecutor' or 'Rescuer' of either party like some 'marshmallow parent' who keeps others dependent and diminished by always rushing to help.

While those around him move from one unofficial role to

another, we see Jesus simply being himself. He remained free. His desire was to rehabilitate, to empower, to create and re-create life by embracing change and generating movement out of stasis. It is not that he was more clever than anyone else, just more transparent. Jesus is pure. He valued Zacchaeus without prejudice or any self-promoting agenda of his own. He did not see a 'sinner' in the tree, nor rejoice to catch some-one out; he did not seize the opportunity to look smart, or make someone else look silly; he did not even capitalize on what could have been a useful moral teaching point. As far as Jesus was concerned, a little man up a tree wanted to be part of everyone else's experience and he responded.

Perhaps Jesus was tired and thirsty. There was nothing patronizing about the way he stated his needs. Maybe, on that hot and crowded day, it was simply that Jesus really did have to shelter somewhere. As on the cross when Jesus told the Roman soldiers he was thirsty, Jesus reached out as one human being to another. The outcome was extraordinary: we see the reformation of Zacchaeus, justice for his victims, and reconciliation for an entire community.

'Salvation has come to this house today' is the statement attributed to Jesus as a tidy ending to the story, yet the reader is left unsure about who has saved who: after all, was Zacchaeus not the one who compensated the crowd and who took Jesus in? There is a satisfying sense of mutuality in this human encounter where everyone gained. Where did Jesus' miracle begin? Not with an accusation, nor even an offer of forgiveness, but with an appeal for help.

The first step to reconciliation, it seems, is to drop labels and to step out of set positions. The crowd labelled Zacchaeus 'sinner'; Jesus rephrased it as 'descendant of Abraham'. Luke called him 'a little man'; Jesus 'looked up' to him. Zacchaeus was marginalized by the crowd; Jesus made himself at home with his family. There is no 'going soft' on sin here. Jesus *ordered* Zacchaeus to come down and face his accusers. He did not collude with Zacchaeus' activities, but he did not reject him either. Remaining in relationship, which involved mutuality of support and hospitality, Zacchaeus retained a sense of dignity and belonging. These made it possible for him to acknowledge his faults and motivated him to make amends without any mud-slinging or humiliation. The response to love is love; the response to condemnation is not always repentance.

In righting wrongs it is not helpful to claim the moral high ground. Roles quickly become reversed and punitive attitudes create an 'us and them' society. Restorative justice schemes like The Sycamore Tree Project, named after this Gospel story, develop dialogue between offenders and their victims in which both sides learn to understand the other. The offender begins to see how crime feels for its victim; the victim sees a human being who may also be wounded. First, both sides need to 'come down' from their positions in order to talk and to listen.

We have all at different stages of our lives been in the tree with Zacchaeus. Avoidance is a very human response. We have also been part of the crowd below, projecting blame on to others and calling people 'sinners' to ease our own sense of shame. There are those who make ready scapegoats – one at least in every playground and workplace, perhaps in every congregation and family home. Jesus does not let any of us off the hook. He continues to call us down from our lofty sense of self-righteousness or from the places we hide from uncomfortable truths. He challenges us to engage with people as they really are. Behind the labels we place on them, we may find that they are not all we assumed them to be. The confident fourfold promise of restitution, for example, suggests that

Zacchaeus may not have cheated anyone. Perhaps the parable that follows this Gospel story was Jesus' way of saying that it is social systems that create injustices rather than the individuals they co-opt.

Whatever we may have done in assigning the varying roles that separate us from other people and from God, Jesus continues to make himself at home 'in our house'. Like Zacchaeus, we must welcome this free spirit who knows our every vantage-point and who refuses to let the opinions of others sway his unconditional regard. We will find that he comes, not to patronize, rescue, collude or condemn, but 'to seek and to save the lost'. It may surprise us, as it did Zacchaeus, to find that we are not the ones doing the seeking after all.

Personal Reflection Time

➤ Whom might I have 'belittled' recently, perhaps without realizing it?

➤ Is there a desire in me for greater inclusion or belonging somewhere?

➤ What kind of 'climbing down' might Jesus be urging me to do?

Prayer

Seek me when I'm lost
Be the guest of this sinner

Confront me when I'm wrong
Be the guest of this sinner

Embrace me when I'm marginalized
Be the guest of this sinner

Come home with me today
Be the guest of this sinner

Open my heart to make amends
Be the guest of this sinner

We pray for . . .

- Victims of fraud
- Marginalized groups
- Reformed offenders

Activities to Consider

❖ Look up instead of down today. When you are outside, notice the trees, rooftops, skies and people's faces.

❖ Try asking for some help if you are usually the one to offer it.

❖ Say sorry to someone you have wronged, misjudged or avoided lately.

9

Within reach

. . . of the housebound

Mark 5.25–34

There was a woman who had suffered terribly from severe bleeding for twelve years, even though she had been treated by many doctors. She had spent all her money, but instead of getting better she got worse all the time. She had heard about Jesus, so she came in the crowd behind him, saying to herself, 'If I just touch his clothes, I will get well.'

She touched his cloak, and her bleeding stopped at once; and she had the feeling inside herself that she was healed of her trouble. At once Jesus knew that power had gone out of him, so he turned round in the crowd and asked, 'Who touched my clothes?'

His disciples answered, 'You see how the people are crowding you; why do you ask who touched you?'

But Jesus kept looking round to see who had done it. The woman realized what had happened to her, so she came, trembling with fear, knelt at his feet, and told him the whole truth. Jesus said to her, 'My daughter, your faith has made you well. Go in peace, and be healed of your trouble.'

A broken arm once seemed the ultimate trophy. I longed to

be surrounded by admiring friends in the school playground and have my plaster covered with get well messages. As a tubby child, injury bravely borne offered a way of raising my social profile. Alas, despite falling from trees and swings quite regularly, I only ever seemed to bounce. How different things are from an adult's perspective. Nowadays, the prospect of serious injury is something to dread.

We all know how easily accidents or ailments can blight a person's life: the implications for quality of life and independence far outweigh any buzz that comes from being the centre of attention. The moment of celebrity passes quickly . . . if it happens at all. Chronic illness leaves a person feeling imprisoned in their own home and marginalized in the community. Some medical conditions impose the extra burden of having to remain hidden. It is difficult, even in our own enlightened times, to talk openly about incontinence, skin disease or 'women's trouble'. It was worse in biblical times when menstrual blood rendered a woman, and anyone she touched, ritually unclean. This woman's chronic condition effectively condemned her to social isolation.

Touching a corpse was also taboo. The Gospel writers had good reason for interweaving this story into the raising of Jairus' daughter. Jesus had deliberately and publicly flouted the ritual purity laws by being in physical contact with a bleeding woman and, minutes later, with a dead child. For any Jew, the whole episode was deeply disturbing, and Jairus, we are told, was particularly respected in the local community. Jesus seemed to be making the point that purity was more than a matter of external ritual.

Christian culture has assimilated the concept of 'clean living'. For some of us, however, 'feeling dirty' has come to describe our whole sense of self. More than feeling guilt for things we have done, we may feel shame about *who we are*.

A sense of unworthiness can incapacitate us as effectively as any medical condition, undermining our confidence, damaging our relationships, and reducing energy for creative or life-giving enterprise. Fear of being 'found out' for who we really are, or for who we are not, becomes a compelling reason for taking a 'no risk' approach to life. Thus, while some people are housebound against their will, others take refuge from society in self-imposed exile. The furtive behaviour of the woman in this story poignantly dramatizes the plight of anyone who feels banished to the margins. At one level it is the story of an ailing woman's miraculous cure: at a deeper level it reads like a penitent's painful confession and absolution.

This miracle of healing seems to have been as much about telling 'the whole truth' as touching Jesus' cloak. Preoccupied as many of us are with our aches and pains, we too may be in need of something much more than a 'clean bill of health'. Jesus desires to heal and cleanse the whole of us – hidden shames, feelings of guilt, and our often chronic lack of self-worth. He was not, as the woman feared, polluted by her supposed uncleanness. The reverse was true: she was cleansed by him. As the woman knelt before him and spilled out her story, we see her trembling with fear at the outrage she anticipated from this man of God. Instead, Jesus addressed her warmly and commended her faith. 'Go in peace', he said.

There is no peace in concealment. Truth sets us free from the terrors of exposure and rejection. Jesus' transparency in this passage contrasts with the woman's avoidant behaviour and fear of detection. Whereas Jesus sensed that something had happened to him and said so, the woman knew for sure that something had happened to her and attempted to keep it quiet. Persisting with his question, 'Who touched my clothes?' Jesus urged her to acknowledge her presence. The healing of this woman is, perhaps, testimony to the humanity of Jesus rather than to any supernatural power. His response in engaging openly with the woman rather than remaining a stranger, and in voicing what he was feeling at the risk of looking foolish, transformed the situation. For her, reaching out for help and revealing her identity were as powerful a statement of self-belief as her faith in Jesus. Truly honest encounters between human beings still work miracles.

Touch does too. The nurse who holds a patient's hand may be more effective than any drug prescribed by the consultant. Reaching out creates a bridge between two people that deeply connects them. By touching him, the woman with the haemorrhage entered Jesus' life. The effect was dramatic and it can be so for us too. But touch must be consensual. Just as Jesus could distinguish between the jostling of the crowd and the touch of this particular woman, he could also draw a distinction between what he freely gave and what was taken from him.

The boundaries of human touch have become the issue of our times. Intimate contact no longer presupposes commitment or even the bond of affection. Jesus' resistance to having something taken from him, even a touch, outside of the context of relationship is a salutary warning to us all. It reminds us that even supportive contact without relationship is not good enough. Cold charity heals no one. A needy person may be content to take or receive impersonal help, but it is our responsibility to add relationship into the equation: there needs to be dignity, space to tell, and mutual acknowledgement.

Ours is a welfare climate where human beings are in danger of becoming 'service users'. It is significant that the woman in this story is nameless. Jesus' response to need was personal, spontaneous and unmeasured. The time he 'wasted' hearing the story of the older woman delayed what urgent help he could extend to Jairus' little daughter, and by the time Jesus got to the child, she was already dead, though he demonstrated a greater miracle by taking the dead girl's hand and raising her to life. The need to prioritize limited time and resources must not distance us from those who try to touch us.

A sense of priority must not hold us back from asking God to help *us*, either. Believing that the starving people of the world are more deserving of God's help, we may be reticent to trouble God with our own needs. We may feel unworthy of his attention. This story of Jesus spending unnecessary time with an unclean woman when he was needed more urgently by an innocent child from a respectable family perhaps demonstrates the unconditional nature of God's compassion. It does not matter who we are, what we have done or how unclean we feel, God has more time for us than we have for him. He sees beyond the presenting issue and desires to hear from us the *whole* truth. He wants us to stop hiding and to kneel at his feet, for he has things to tell us too: that we are his child and that our faith in his love will keep us well. What starts out in prayer as a specific urgent request may end up as a reassurance of our worth as human beings. Peace may be the answer, as it was for the woman, to a prayer we never voiced.

Jesus the bountiful giver was not unaffected by his giving and healing. This story makes it clear that he knew what it felt like to be drained. Ultimately, of course, his selflessness cost him his life. Even before that point, he experienced the range of emotions and physical sensations any other human being knows. Instances of his extraordinary insights into human nature are complemented by examples, as in this passage, of apparent cluelessness: 'Jesus kept looking round to see who had done it.'

Most poignant of all is his sudden sense that 'power had

gone out of him'. It happened at the same time that the woman felt an inner conviction that she had been healed. She had spent 20 years feeling her life drain away: now Jesus took that feeling from her and experienced it personally. Such empathy is rarely known by human beings, except perhaps by parents. Often a mother or father may cry out, 'If only I could bear this instead', for this is the child they brought into the world and love more than their own life. How else do we imagine God feels towards us? How else would he respond to our pain but as a father to his child? 'My daughter,' Jesus said to the woman . . .

Personal Reflection Time

➢ What drains me?

➢ Is there anyone trying to 'touch' or engage with me whom I am failing to notice?

➢ Which aspects of myself do I withhold from people?

Prayer

> With faith in your mercy
> **I touch you, Lord**
>
> With faith in your time for me
> **I touch you, Lord**
>
> With faith in your love for me
> **I touch you, Lord**
>
> With faith in your forgiveness
> **I touch you, Lord**

With compassion for myself
I touch you, Lord

We pray for . . .

- AIDS sufferers

- The chronically ill

- Exhausted carers

Activities to Consider

❖ In your next conversation, practise telling the whole truth rather than a version of it.

❖ Give some practical help to anyone who seems drained at the moment.

❖ Hold an object or garment that belongs to someone you love whom you cannot get close to at the moment. Pray for them.

10

Within reach

... of the bereaved

John 11.1, 3–6, 11, 20–27

*A man named Lazarus, who lived in Bethany, was ill.
Bethany was the town where Mary and her sister Martha
lived ... The sisters sent Jesus a message: 'Lord, your dear
friend is ill.'*

*When Jesus heard it, he said, 'The final result of this ill-
ness will not be the death of Lazarus; this has happened in
order to bring glory to God, and it will be the means by
which the Son of God will receive glory.'*

*Jesus loved Martha and her sister and Lazarus. Yet when
he received the news that Lazarus was ill, he stayed where
he was for two more days ...*

*Jesus said this and then added, 'Our friend Lazarus has
fallen asleep, but I will go and wake him up.'*

*When Martha heard that Jesus was coming, she went out
to meet him, but Mary stayed in the house. Martha said to
Jesus, 'If you had been here, Lord, my brother would not
have died! But I know that even now God will give you
whatever you ask him for.'*

'Your brother will rise to life,' Jesus told her.

'I know,' she replied, 'that he will rise to life on the last day.'

Jesus said to her, 'I am the resurrection and the life. Whoever believes in me will live, even though he dies; and whoever lives and believes in me will never die. Do you believe this?'

'Yes, Lord!' she answered. 'I do believe that you are the Messiah, the Son of God, who was to come into the world.'

Working for six years on a prison chaplaincy team offered me plenty of scope for Christian service. It therefore came as a hurtful rebuff when someone teased, 'Why don't you wear roller skates and go around with a notice saying, "Here to help"?' The sting of this remark forced me to think hard about the extent to which I was helping or hindering. I had to acknowledge that it is not a service of love to indulge people or to collude with learned helplessness. I had to accept, for myself as well as for others, that it may be good for us some-times to go without; to reassess what we really need; to be able to wait and to take responsibility for ourselves. There are times, of course, when all of us need support – proud or stubborn independence is not the alternative to dependency. *Inter*-dependence is.

The way we pray can be very enlightening about our view of what help is or what love really means. As always, the way we relate to God reflects our pattern of relating to other people. Loving us does not oblige God to surrender to our will. As any responsible parent will know, love must sometimes be 'tough love', and simply say 'no'. Our relationship with God is not an equal relationship between adults, for God is God and we are his children, but he does encourage us to grow and mature in prayer beyond infantile sleeve tugging. Jesus is not a critical response unit any more than he is our pet or talisman, yet we so often try to make him an emergency helpline to get us out of scrapes and save us from the consequences of our actions. He is there to help, care and guide, but in the context of a relationship that already exists and is growing, one in which we take our own full and active part.

There was nothing inappropriate about Mary's and Martha's desperate plea for help, which makes it all the more shocking to read of Jesus' negative response to the news that his friend was ill. The sisters evidently believed he would respond with immediate assistance and openly acknowledged their disappointment with him. It reminds us of times when we too have begged for divine intervention. There is something familiar about the delay between an urgent request for help and Jesus' response. As with Martha, we may feel a sense of betrayal until the lapse of time brings awareness of God's undetected but very watchful presence in difficult situations. '. . . for your sake,' Jesus told his disciples, 'I am glad that I was not with him, so that you will believe' (John 11.15). Prayers are always answered, but we do not necessarily realize how.

We may speculate why Jesus refused to respond to the news that Lazarus was seriously ill. For one thing he was lying low on the other side of the Jordan, in danger of his own life. Even an immediate departure could not have got him there before Lazarus died. What is important for us to take in was that Jesus was not on earth to prolong life, but to teach the purpose of life. The raising of Lazarus from the dead was an answer to prayer at a deeper level than physical rescue.

Jesus' conversation with Martha gently led her beyond a concern for the immediate and the material. On meeting her at the entrance to the village, Jesus heard but did not react to her blaming statement, 'if you had been here, Lord, my brother would not have died!' Instead he offered hope for the future, 'Your brother will rise to life,' as well as a more meaningful relationship for her in the here and now, 'I am the resurrection and the life.' Life both now and for eternity were to be found in Jesus.

Martha was able to move on to this spiritual plane. She had learned that faith is not about the 'delivery of goods' like cures or miracles; it is about growth in a relationship that makes life on earth fuller and more meaningful. Biological death is a transition towards the fulfilment of a quality of loving and living that our earthly experience has begun to open up for us. In Martha's reawakening to the possibility that lay before her, the miracle had already taken place. The physical raising of Lazarus was almost a separate story.

God does not allow us to suffer in order to draw deep insights from every personal tragedy. After all, Jesus taught us in 'The Lord's Prayer' to ask our heavenly Father for deliverance from bad things happening to us. Nevertheless, God uses our struggles to coax us towards a closer relationship with him and, by extension, with ourselves and others. We need not worry about bringing to God what seem very petty personal concerns, as long as in them all we are learning and growing.

There are times when we become the answer to our prayers: the Creator may generate something new in us to transform a 'problem' into a life-changing re-direction. At other times he gives over and above what we ask. He may, of course, answer us with a firm but loving 'no', as he did to Jesus when he prayed in the garden that the cup of suffering might be taken away from him. Very often the answer to prayer is not what we expect, for our imagination is limited and we cannot grasp the wealth of possibility at God's disposal. For Martha and Mary it would have been miracle enough to cure Lazarus of a life-threatening condition . . . they hardly expected Jesus to raise him from the dead. Waiting for an answer, as they had to do, is a common experience for Christians. God's timescale is different from ours.

In this story of a developing dialogue between Martha and Jesus we see all these elements of initial disappointment, learning through waiting, as well as answers above and beyond our wildest expectations. The greater miracle, perhaps, was the insight into what resurrection really means. Learning to pray teaches us how to live with God for eternity. Just as we learn that God wants to be more to us than a dispenser of favours on request, so we realize that resurrection is more than resuscitation. It is not the continuation of life 'in heaven as it is on earth', but the other way round – the start of life 'on earth as it is in heaven'. Often we are too preoccupied with self to feel as alive as Jesus was. Life to its full potential involves a losing and a regaining of ourselves in the same kind of way that the death and raising of Lazarus symbolized.

Life is to be found in the same relationship which Jesus enjoyed with his Father – that continual mutual exchange of love and honour, where personal loss as we know it no longer inflicts such devastating impact, where whoever 'believes . . . will never die'. Life need no longer be imprisoned within the boundaries of that ever-demanding sense of self, of neediness and greediness, of insecurity and desire. When we learn to transform existence into living, then dying will hold less terror. Life is not breathing, getting, competing, surviving, but . . . appreciating, valuing, wondering, connecting, sharing and glorifying. When we finally come to understand that resurrection life is not a thing, nor a condition, nor a place nor something to be had, but a person whose own life in God we are invited to share, then we will fear death and darkness a little less. It is then that we can begin to walk by a different kind of light to the world's light.

Personal Reflection Time

➤ What is my reply to Jesus' question, 'I am the resurrection and the life . . . Do you believe this?'

➤ Which of my relationships with living people – and which parts of myself – need to be brought back to life?

➤ Using Martha's statement from the passage, 'I do believe that you are the Messiah, the Son of God, who was to come into the world', replace the words 'the world' with as many examples as you can from your own personal circumstances:

> e.g. I believe that you are the Messiah, the Son of God, who was to come into 'my attempts to get a job'

Prayer

> Faith has no end
> **I believe**
>
> Hope has no end
> **I believe**
>
> Love has no end
> **I believe**

We remember those who may die . . .

- un-mourned
- un-reconciled
- un-believing

Activities to Consider

❖ Take some flowers to the grave of a loved one. You might take a brush to spruce up the headstone. Say a prayer. If you have time, tidy up a neglected grave nearby.

❖ Resurrect something you no longer use by recycling it in a creative way, restoring it or giving it to someone who needs it more.

❖ Consider lending a treasured book or film to someone else.

11

Within reach

. . . of the blind

Luke 18.31–43

Jesus took the twelve disciples aside and said to them, 'Listen! We are going to Jerusalem where everything the prophets wrote about the Son of Man will come true. He will be handed over to the Gentiles, who will mock him, insult him, and spit on him. They will whip him, and kill him, but three days later he will rise to life.'

But the disciples did not understand any of these things; the meaning of the words was hidden from them, and they did not know what Jesus was talking about.

As Jesus was coming near Jericho, there was a blind man sitting by the road, begging. When he heard the crowd passing by, he asked, 'What is this?'

'Jesus of Nazareth is passing by,' they told him.

He cried out, 'Jesus! Son of David! Take pity on me!'

The people in front scolded him and told him to be quiet. But he shouted even more loudly, 'Son of David! Take pity on me!'

So Jesus stopped and ordered the blind man to be brought to him. When he came near, Jesus asked him, 'What do you want me to do for you?'

'Sir,' he answered, 'I want to see again.'

Jesus said to him, 'Then see! Your faith has made you well.'

At once he was able to see, and he followed Jesus, giving thanks to God. When the crowd saw it, they all praised God.

Not being allowed in to play in Sandra's tent next door seemed a big issue to me as a small child. I could make out shadowy figures within and hear the excited voices of the bigger children. Even though I could not see what they were doing, I desperately wanted to be part of it. Eventually they would open the flap to let me in, but I learned at an early age that there is nothing more humiliating and frustrating than feeling left out, especially from the experiences of older siblings who may be unwilling to share or let us into secrets. Being hushed is another familiar experience for children.

Some people never do manage to join in or get anyone to hear what they have to say. Bartimaeus, as he is called in Mark's Gospel, 'heard the crowd passing by' but was not part of what was going on. It is not just blindness which creates situations like this. Language difficulties or mobility needs, sometimes the deliberate unkindness of other people, can mean that we too may feel excluded from communal activities. Christmas festivities or the sound of a summer barbecue in someone's garden, which offer such pleasure to people with family and friends, may be exquisite torture for a lonely neighbour.

A breakdown in our relationship with God may feel like the ultimate exclusion, especially at times of the Church's year when God's love is being celebrated. The 'crowd' of church-goers may place conditions on God's apparent accessibility or, by their particular way of expressing faith, repel us from the person of Jesus. Luke tells us that it was 'the people in front' who rebuked Bartimaeus. Leaders in our own church circles may be the very ones who block the spiritual progress of others. The 'crowd', of course, may instead turn out to be critical voices inside our own heads: self-rejecting thoughts, unacknowledged shames, and ever-growing lists of 'things to do' that push us further and further from God.

Bartimaeus' urgent appeal over the heads of the crowd was a plea for something more than money. Even in this matter-of-fact written account, we catch the desperation in his voice. He evidently wanted to be heard, forgiven, and to be fully part of the worshipping community. In this sense, Bartimaeus represents us all. We are all at some time in our lives unable to feel part of what is going on and begging to be noticed and included.

It does not take long to appreciate the irony in this passage: in calling Jesus 'Son of David', the blind man turned out to be the only Jericho citizen who was *not* blind. Bartimaeus was hailing Jesus as true King of the Jews and, by that, he meant a king like David, close enough to God to be seated in his presence, a shepherd-king who served and suffered with his people. Herod Antipas, who currently occupied the throne, was neither descended from King David, nor resembled him in his actions. It may not have been prudent for Bartimaeus to question the legitimacy of Herod's rule at the top of his voice in the street – no wonder the crowd tried to hush him!

Jesus did not hush him. Perhaps, like Bartimaeus, he also felt alone in the crowd. The disciples who were his constant companions had evidently failed to comprehend Jesus or his mission. We read in the preamble to the Bartimaeus story that they did not understand or accept his patient explanation of this last journey up to Jerusalem where he expected to suffer and to die. What a lonely last journey it must have seemed for him, unable to share his sadness and dread with his closest friends. Then suddenly Bartimaeus was calling . . . someone who actually understood. Jesus welcomed the lone prophetic voice across the crowd and insisted on meeting the person – perhaps the *only* person – who could really *see*.

When Jesus asked, 'What do you want me to do for you?', Bartimaeus did not ask for any material support. In the first instance he did not even ask for healing. We might reflect on our own answer to Jesus' question. What do *we* want? Do we beg that life's immediate frustrations might be taken away, or are we, on reflection, desiring that something more fundamental should change within us? Bartimaeus asked for compassion. Only later he asked for sight. It was a brave request. He would no longer have a legitimate reason to beg. In material terms he could end up much worse off, for the whole of Jericho witnessed his recovery.

Jesus gave him what he asked. He also acknowledged Bartimaeus' own part in his healing. 'Your faith has made you well,' he said. What can he have meant but Bartimaeus' persistence, his recognition of Jesus' true identity, his understanding of the connection between forgiveness and healing, and his irrepressible belief in Jesus' willingness to reach out to people. One wonders whether God also granted Bartimaeus what he could have asked for but decided not to, such as the means of supporting himself and the respect of the local community who had witnessed his act of faith. The scripture only tells us, however, that he 'followed Jesus, giving thanks to God'. It was a road that led shortly to Calvary.

This story stretches our understanding of the kingdom that Jesus preached. We come to appreciate that sight is more about faith and understanding than about the physical ability to see; that healing is more about forgiveness, peace of mind and reconciliation than about physical cures or prolongation of life. Bartimaeus' following of Jesus reflects a deep conversion of life more than a joyous relief at changed circumstances, for in many ways these circumstances must have been, materially speaking, a change for the worse. His conversion must already have begun as he picked up what people were saying about Jesus, otherwise he would not so confidently have hailed him as Son of David. Talk of Jesus had perhaps already opened his eyes to the need for mercy, and made him determined to pursue the quest to find Jesus for himself, no matter who tried to stand in his way. His gratitude was of the kind that sealed an enduring bond with the restorer of his sight and generated an infectious sense of God's goodness . . . 'When the crowd saw it, they *all* praised God.'

If we were begging by the roadside that day, if we were one of the disciples or if we were cheering in the crowd, would we have been asking for favours, urging him to abandon his dangerous plan and basking in his celebrity status? Or would we, like the solitary figure of Bartimaeus, have been able to give up a lifetime's work of asking and start to give instead? Following Jesus is unlikely to lead to our martyrdom, but it might mean making material comfort less of a priority. We may even find this a liberating change and, like Bartimaeus, begin to praise God for 'opening our eyes' to the good things of life. Jesus understood that reaching Jericho meant nearing the end of his earthly life. What do we want to ask of Jesus that will equip us for the ascending road to our own Jerusalem?

Personal Reflection Time

➢ Draw a 'road map' or time-line of your own life so far. At which points were you closest to Jesus?

➢ Praise God for any new insights he has given you today.

➢ What is today's reply to Jesus' question, 'What do you want me to do for you?'

Prayer

> I am blind to my own faults
> **Lord, I want to see**
>
> I am blind to others' needs
> **Lord, I want to see**
>
> I am blind to your presence
> **Lord, I want to see**
>
> I believe you can heal me
> **Lord, I want to see**

We remember before God . . .

- Those without eyesight

- Those without income

- Those without long to live

Activities to Consider

❖ Find a place such as a window or park bench where you can sit for a while (as long as it feels safe and is not too cold). Watch the world go by . . .

❖ Decide on a charity you can support regularly, if you do not already have one. Find out more about its work.

❖ Think of anyone you have recently told (or wanted to tell) to 'shut up'. Consider going back to ask them what they were trying to say.

12

Within reach

. . . of the stranger

John 12.20–33

Some Greeks were among those who had gone to Jerusalem to worship during the festival. They went to Philip (he was from Bethsaida in Galilee) and said, 'Sir, we want to see Jesus.'

Philip went and told Andrew, and the two of them went and told Jesus. Jesus answered them, 'The hour has now come for the Son of Man to receive great glory. I am telling you the truth: a grain of wheat remains no more than a single grain unless it is dropped into the ground and dies. If it does die, then it produces many grains. Whoever loves his own life will lose it; whoever hates his own life in this world will keep it for life eternal. Whoever wants to serve me must follow me, so that my servant will be with me where I am. And my Father will honour anyone who serves me.

'Now my heart is troubled – and what shall I say? Shall I say, "Father, do not let this hour come upon me"? But that is why I came – so that I might go through this hour of suffering. Father, bring glory to your name!'

Then a voice spoke from heaven, 'I have brought glory to it, and I will do so again.' The crowd standing there heard the voice, and some of them said it was thunder, while others said, 'An angel spoke to him!'

But Jesus said to them, 'It was not for my sake that this voice spoke, but for yours. Now is the time for this world to be judged; now the ruler of this world will be overthrown. When I am lifted up from the earth, I will draw everyone to me.' (In saying this he indicated the kind of death he was going to suffer.)

Ancient Greeks were indefatigable seekers after Truth. Sophisticated people, they travelled widely and were fascinated by the world of ideas and beliefs. These particular 'Greeks' may have been converts to Judaism come to worship at the Feast, or perhaps, as believers in many gods, they were 'doing the rounds' of religious sites. They may not actually have come from Greece itself – the term 'Greeks' applied generally to the non-Jewish peoples of the Mediterranean world – but they evidently approached Philip first because he had a Greek name. Philip did not feel very sure about them. Perhaps he feared that they had no real understanding of the Jewish faith, or maybe he was suspicious of foreigners. Whatever his misgivings, Andrew evidently persuaded him to pass on their request to Jesus.

This moment of Jesus' ministry when Gentile peoples said, 'we want to see Jesus,' seems to have been one of poignant personal significance. Though his ministry had touched the lives of various non-Jews, his mission was primarily to God's 'chosen people', the Jewish nation itself. It was to be his disciples' mission to carry the light of revelation to the furthest reaches of the pagan world when, 'lifted up' on the cross and from the tomb, Jesus would draw everyone to himself. Perhaps the appearance of Greeks insistent upon seeing him emphasized to Jesus that his own earthly ministry was drawing to a close: 'The hour has now come', he said. The Greeks' quest to find life signified the moment when Jesus himself would face death. We sense his mixed emotions, a sense both of the triumphant fulfilment of his mission, coupled with feelings of dread at the thought of the suffering that awaited him.

The connection between glory and suffering seems, however, to have been lost on Jesus' disciples. Jesus had, after all, entered Jerusalem in triumph. The Gospel writer describes in the preceding passage how crowds of people greeted him, waving palm branches and shouting 'Hosanna!' It was this excitement no doubt that prompted the Greek visitors to find out more about this man who was the talk of Jerusalem. The disciples must have felt that their hopes for Jesus to sweep to prominence had been vindicated. Jesus had to spell it out yet again that, in order for the enemies of God's Kingdom to be overcome, Jesus must be lifted up in crucifixion, not raised to power.

Like the disciples, we understand glory in very different terms from the glory Jesus was trying to describe. For us, glory is about our own reputation, about being lifted a little above other people by exciting their envy or admiration. Jesus was trying to explain that glory was not about superiority, but about service. It was not about him or us: Jesus could only see glory in relation to God's glory. His own glory was to reveal the Father. Revealing God meant delivering God's message of love and mercy even to the point of suffering death at the hands of those who resisted it. Being 'lifted up' for the whole world to see and understand God's love also, in starker terms, described the most barbaric form of Roman execution.

Like the Greek tourists, we do not want to 'miss out' on any sensational spiritual opportunities. Like them, we may approach those we think can give us access to a more direct experience of God, whether it is by following great preachers, attending charismatic gatherings, emulating inspiring people, seeking spiritual direction, or praying through the saints. The request is essentially the same: we want to see Jesus. Jesus' response, though, may be disconcerting.

We are not told whether the Greeks were granted their personal interview. Possibly not, for a later verse tells us that, 'he went off and hid himself from them' (John 12.36). It is as if Jesus was saying, you *will* see me in a day or two, hanging on a cross for all to stare at to their hearts' content. He is perhaps saying the same to us: 'You say you would like to see me? You *do* see me all the time. The cross is everywhere you look – on silver chains round people's necks, displayed over church doorways, in the events of your own and others' lives. But, more especially, wherever there is hardship, pain, loss, sorrow or injustice, there you will see me. I came to share it with you.'

We cannot avoid the sight of the cross if we truly desire to see Jesus. We cannot edit the story and keep just the 'nice' bits any more than we can edit our own story and live in denial of all the shames, losses and fearful situations we have experienced, and will experience in the future. Some people try to, of course. They pick and choose – even re-write – what they wish to remember, and hide from things they will not, or feel they cannot, face. In the end reality catches up with us: shames become known, ageing processes accelerate, and eventually death overtakes us all.

Jesus feared suffering, but faced up to the destiny that awaited him. Like Jesus, our own glory is not to be found in successfully dodging anything that might expose or hurt us. Transcending our fears, we find glory in engaging with the difficulties of life in a way that brings light and life to others and that bears out the truth of God's love and mercy to a desperately waiting world. We too are called to be the wheat that falls to the ground and dies in order to produce many grains. The glory is in spending – not saving – ourselves.

Many who would not describe themselves as Christians would go along with much of Jesus' teachings about social justice. It is when it comes to the cross that true Christians part company with spiritual 'tourists'. Embracing death is a controversial idea. Seeing Jesus hanging on a cross is not the context in which most people desire to see him. We would rather see him welcoming little children, multiplying loaves, healing lepers, and transfigured in heavenly light. Jesus in agony, Jesus flogged, Jesus spat upon, Jesus defeated . . . these are not what we have in mind when we say, 'we want to see Jesus'. The crowds who jostled for a glimpse of him on Palm Sunday no longer desired to see him a few days later when he was nailed to a cross in full public view.

It is interesting how differently people interpreted the voice from heaven when Jesus openly acknowledged that his heart was troubled. Some heard thunder; others, the voice of an angel. We are no different. At the mention of suffering, we hear either thunder or angels: either we dread and fear suffering, or we are able to perceive God's involvement in our lives. It is when hardship strikes us that our readiness to follow our suffering Saviour is tested.

I am reminded of one of our Sisters who recently died of cancer. Working for many years as a nurse, she was a channel of Christian love to innumerable patients. Yet it was her own dying that can best be described as glorious, suffering uncomplainingly and, despite her discomfort, thinking of others more than herself. Not many people would encourage their doctor at the end of a long shift to go home and see to her in the morning.

The voice from heaven revealed to an incredulous crowd the relationship Jesus had with his heavenly Father. Our readiness to engage with the sometimes trying realities of life is the means God chooses for us to develop and reveal the quality of our relationship with him. How we engage with hardship and pain affects not only ourselves. Just as the voice from heaven was, as Jesus said, 'not for my sake . . . but for yours', the way we behave in response to our troubled hearts may have a significance that extends far beyond the confines of our own little world.

Personal Reflection Time

➤ Thank God for any 'lifting' experiences recently.

➤ Looking back over the last few days, at which times did I 'see Jesus' most clearly?

➤ What examples of self-sacrifice do I see around me that bring glory to God?

Prayer

In my living
Be glorified

In my worshipping
Be glorified

In my sharing
Be glorified

In my serving
Be glorified

In my dying
Be glorified

We remember before God . . .

- Visitors to our country
- Newcomers to our church
- Heroes in our community

Activities to Consider

❖ Plant something for a person you know who is suffering at the moment. Remember to say a prayer for them every time you water the plant or look at it.

❖ Show support for someone you know whose 'heart is troubled' or who faces a difficult future.

❖ Make a special effort to welcome strangers at church.

13

Within reach

. . . of the traitor

John 18.1–10

After Jesus had said this prayer, he left with his disciples and went across the brook called Kidron. There was a garden in that place, and Jesus and his disciples went in. Judas, the traitor, knew where it was, because many times Jesus had met there with his disciples. So Judas went to the garden, taking with him a group of Roman soldiers, and some temple guards sent by the chief priests and the Pharisees; they were armed and carried lanterns and torches. Jesus knew everything that was going to happen to him, so he stepped forward and asked them, 'Who is it you are looking for?'

'Jesus of Nazareth,' they answered.

'I am he,' he said.

Judas, the traitor, was standing there with them. When Jesus said to them, 'I am he,' they moved back and fell to the ground. Again Jesus asked them, 'Who is it you are looking for?'

'Jesus of Nazareth,' they said.

'I have already told you that I am he,' Jesus said. 'If, then, you are looking for me, let these others go.' (He said this so

*that what he had said might come true: 'Father, I have not
lost even one of those you gave me.')*

*Simon Peter, who had a sword, drew it and struck the
High Priest's slave, cutting off his right ear. The name of the
slave was Malchus. Jesus said to Peter, 'Put your sword back
in its place! Do you think that I will not drink the cup of
suffering which my Father has given me?'*

Jesus and his disciples must often have withdrawn to this quiet
garden. No doubt it was in sombre mood that they left the
upper room after sharing the Passover meal together. Their
familiar walk to the Mount of Olives from the city went down
through the Kidron brook, which at Passover time ran red
with the blood of lambs slaughtered for sacrifice: it perhaps
reminded Jesus of the fate awaiting him.

The disciples, however, still failed to grasp that this terrible
danger was not one that Jesus could avert. Perhaps their
naïvety increased his sense of loneliness and abandonment.
He cannot have been in a peaceful frame of mind. We read
that, overcome by the grim and now very imminent prospect
of crucifixion, he threw himself upon the ground and prayed
to be spared. Fear made him feverish and panicky – he expressed irritation at the disciples who kept dozing off while he
was praying in desperation to his heavenly Father.

The process of wrestling alone in prayer brought him eventually to the kind of serenity that only submission to the will
of the Father can bring. It was not the peace of exhaustion,
nor the peace of the garden. It was the peace of doing what
he had to do, of doing the right thing. For Jesus, this was the
decision to place everything in the hands of the Father. 'Do
you think that I will not drink the cup of suffering which my
Father has given me?' he was able to say when Peter tried to
resist the arresting officers. So it was that, when Judas arrived

with Roman troops and temple police, Jesus showed no urge
to put up a fight or run for it.

What a contrast to that other garden, the Garden of Eden,
where, in the cool of the day, God went looking for man, and
man hid for shame. Now the roles were reversed: in the cool
of a very different day, many men went searching for God. Yet
Jesus did not hide for shame or run away in fear: he 'stepped
forward' and acknowledged 'I am he'. There is a peace in just
being who we are and not someone else, just as there is peace
in accepting our circumstances, however trying they might be,
and not trying to escape them or to avoid the consequences of
our own decisions. There is peace in taking responsibility for
ourselves and not blaming someone else.

Jesus' question, 'Who is it you are looking for?' is a strange
one, given that he was anticipating capture. Jesus was not
feigning surprise or playing for time like we might be tempted
to do. Though he may not have been prepared to defend himself physically, he was not going to collude with their unlawful
arrest. In forcing them to state their business, he showed his
authority. Perhaps the size of the force surprised him. Jesus
was not naïve, but he must have been astonished that Roman
troops were despatched to help the temple guards bring him
in. He was not 'General Jesus', simply Jesus from Nazareth.

Jesus' perception of himself, and the perception other people
had of him, were evidently very different. The Pharisees saw
him as a heretic instilling wrong-headedness into the minds
of susceptible followers; the authorities saw him as a trouble-
maker likely to endanger their fragile working relationship
with the Roman occupying forces. Even his disciples hoped
he might usher in a kingdom to overthrow foreign rule. As far
as Judas was concerned, Jesus' pacifism amounted to betrayal.
Yet the kingdom Jesus spoke of had never been the kind of
kingdom his followers and his opponents imagined. Jesus

dreamed of the kind of society where relationships between people were just and where God ruled over human hearts. This kind of dreaming had nothing to do with swords.

Jesus asked the question twice of the arresting force. He continues to ask it of us: 'Who is it you are looking for?' Some of us are still looking for the wrong man. We still want him to seize power, to overthrow our enemies by force, to rescue us from the things that oppress and diminish us, and to take responsibility for bad things that we contribute to but feel powerless to prevent. Just like Judas, we blame him for not being willing to take action and fight our battles for us. Just like the crowds, we try to push Jesus into a kind of kingship he did not want to take; at the same time, just like the Jewish authorities, we blame him when his moral authority poses a threat to the sovereignty we jealously guard over our own lives. We were all represented in the garden at that moment in the dead of night on that first Maundy Thursday: you and I were the dozing disciples in denial, the traitorous Judas full of pretended affection, the soldiers anxious to tie Jesus up and make him a scapegoat. Potentially, you and I are also the plain-speaking honest men and women of integrity who step forward and are willing to say, 'This is who I am' – or even, 'Yes, I am the culprit'.

People throughout the ages have somehow felt the need to track God down. Those on retreat sometimes come with their equivalent of lanterns and torches as though Jesus might evade them. There is no need for a search-party. Some people approach prayer in the same coercive way as the soldiers who came armed with weapons – not just outlining their need, but directing God how to meet it. Jesus tells us, as he told Peter, to put our swords back in the scabbard and to stop trying to *make* things happen. Worse still, we may approach Jesus as Judas did. Judas' kiss, referred to in the other three Gospels, turned out to be a false show of affection: it was the signal he had agreed to use to identify Jesus. Do we, too, approach Jesus with words of intimacy when in our hearts we feel something quite different? Do we try to 'soft-soap' God in the hope of getting what we want?

It is a moving moment when Jesus states, 'I am he'. Jesus was showing authority. Some would say that he was using the name by which God was called. The party – or some of them perhaps – fell to the ground. We must be mindful whom we are approaching when we pray. We may not prostrate ourselves, but we need at least to enter a new state of awareness as we dare to address God's Son. We must put down our swords – and our lanterns and torches – and hesitate to greet him as an intimate friend if there is any hint of betrayal or falseness in the words or gestures we use. We must come to God as he comes to us, in peace, in honesty. We need to acknowledge that he is who he is, and not someone of our own making. We need to be sure that we are who we are and not pretending to be someone else.

How we are with God tells us a great deal about how we are with other people. So often we come against them armed and menacing, seeking to shine a torch into their lives, to accuse them of misdeeds, and to take control. We offer them a kiss in friendship then plot to bring them down. Just as Peter assaulted the High Priest's slave instead of the High Priest who sent him, the ones we accuse are rarely the people who really hurt us. Again and again Jesus asks us, 'Who is it you are looking for?' and orders us to 'let these others go'. We need not make our own gardens into a battlefield.

Personal Reflection Time

> ➤ Recall an episode in which you have reacted aggressively or defensively. Ask Jesus to help you to 'Put your sword back in its place'.

> ➤ Jesus prayed, 'Father, I have not lost even one of those you gave me.' How does it feel to be entrusted into Jesus' care?

> ➤ Jesus met in this private garden 'many times . . . with his disciples'. What kind of place feels safe and special for you? Imagine yourself there with Jesus.

Prayer

I am looking for . . .

Someone to challenge me
Jesus, you are he

Someone to restrain me
Jesus, you are he

Someone to defend me
Jesus, you are he

Someone to forgive me
Jesus, you are he

Someone to keep me safe
Jesus, you are he

We pray for . . .

- Victims of knife crime
- Victims of religious hatred
- Victims of false allegations

Activities to Consider

❖ Experiment with different prayer postures. Some companions of Judas lay face down before Jesus . . . you might try that too.

❖ Consider supporting an organization that promotes peace. You can find out more about Pax Christi at www.paxchristi.org.uk.

❖ Make a special effort to greet people warmly with a kiss or handshake that you really mean.

14

Within reach

. . . of the friend

John 18.15–18; Luke 22.58–62

Simon Peter and another disciple followed Jesus. That other disciple was well known to the High Priest, so he went with Jesus into the courtyard of the High Priest's house, while Peter stayed outside by the gate. Then the other disciple went back out, spoke to the girl at the gate, and brought Peter inside. The girl at the gate said to Peter, 'Aren't you also one of the disciples of that man?'

'No, I am not,' answered Peter.

It was cold, so the servants and guards had built a charcoal fire and were standing round it, warming themselves. So Peter went over and stood with them, warming himself . . .

. . . After a little while a man noticed Peter and said, 'You are one of them, too!'

But Peter answered, 'Man, I am not!'

And about an hour later another man insisted strongly, 'There isn't any doubt that this man was with Jesus, because he also is a Galilean!'

But Peter answered, 'Man, I don't know what you are talking about!'

At once, while he was still speaking, a cock crowed. The

Lord turned round and looked straight at Peter, and Peter remembered that the Lord had said to him, 'Before the cock crows tonight, you will say three times that you do not know me.' Peter went out and wept bitterly.

We will never know to what lengths Peter had gone that night to reach Jesus. He had put up a stout defence of his Master at the time of the arrest and, later on, had somehow managed to gain access to the High Priest's house. Perhaps he hoped to glean information, but when he overheard the determination of Jesus' accusers and saw the numbers of temple guards and officials, he must have realized that any rescue attempt was futile. Peter's nerve had failed once before when he tried to walk on water to meet his Master across the waves. On that occasion Jesus had stretched out a hand to save him. This time, Jesus' hands were chained. He could only reach out to Peter with his eyes.

Peter's denial that he ever knew Jesus is a story that features in all four Gospels. It was embarrassing adverse publicity for the man whom Jesus had nominated as the head of his Church. Believers would remember him for all time as the friend who boasted fidelity to Jesus yet who, for fear of arrest, was not even present at his crucifixion. After three years of studying peace and love, we see Peter going about armed with a sword. We read that, only metres away from where Jesus stuck to the truth under brutal interrogation, Peter was warming himself at a fire and telling lies. The only thing that gave him away as a disciple was . . . his Galilean accent.

The Gospels may paint an inglorious portrait of Peter, but Christians through the ages have not condemned him. They, like Jesus, have 'looked straight at Peter' and felt only compassion. There is a capacity within us all for passionate outspokenness and rock-like dependability, yet there is also a 'shadow' side, the part of us that reneges on our own beliefs and occasionally strikes out viciously (as Peter did when he cut off the servant's ear) at people with whom we have no real quarrel. Firelight casts flickering and distorted shadows. His own shadow across the High Priest's courtyard must have seemed, to Peter, grotesque.

Self-realization can be very painful. Peter's extravagant statement, 'I am ready to die for you' (John 13.37), had been shown up to be an empty boast. Underneath the physical strength, resourcefulness and bluster were fear and the same instinct we all have for self-preservation. There are times in our lives when bravado and self-deception can no longer disguise some hideous truth about our shallowness or selfishness, our cowardice or treachery. Peter had reached this place and we are told that he wept bitterly. For us, too, moments of humiliation, shame or exposure can feel as though our world has come to an end. All that has come to an end is the legend we create about ourselves.

Jesus is never taken in by the outward persona, so he is never shocked when we show a 'different side to us'. He knows that the so-called 'shadow' self is as much 'us' as the sociable side that we present to the world. Jesus 'looks straight' at us in an unconditional acceptance of who we are. He takes in the whole, and helps us to look at ourselves and others in the same direct but loving way. Just as cockcrow jolted Peter to an awareness of the way he had denied his Master, Jesus wakens us to painful self-truths. His motive is not to bring us down but to begin our healing.

Reaching a place of honesty in a context of love and self-forgiveness makes it possible for us to integrate the good and bad sides of our nature and to become more 'real'. Peter was described as the rock on which the Church could be built, but for Peter to be strong, he had first to be authentic. Giving up the pretence of being someone we are not releases energy. Accepting both our giftedness and our limitations can free us to be inter-dependent and relieve us of burdens too great for us to bear alone. Awareness of our actual sinfulness as well as our potential for saintliness keeps us close to God, the source of our life, our creativity and our growth. Our whole concept of success can be redefined to allow for our humanity.

Re-orientation for Peter had been a long and painful process. The faith of his childhood had had to assimilate some new and radical ideas. It must have been a daily struggle to integrate his experience of Jesus' transfiguration and miracles into what the Master was trying to teach about the Saviour who must suffer and die. His eyes had to be opened, too, to truths about himself, such as his own fallibility and neediness. That was another kind of dying he had to accept. We can imagine a quieter, humbler Peter back home in Galilee following the death of Jesus, trying to resume his old business amid a community that perhaps laughed at his shamefaced reappearance.

We read about Peter's re-birth in the post-resurrection story of John 21. It gives a mirror-image of the painful episode in the High Priest's courtyard. Out in the boat, the disciples were guided to a shoal of fish by a figure on the lakeside. Throwing the net to the other side of the boat at his direction, the disciples found they had netted a gigantic catch. Perhaps the number of fish reminded Peter of that other miraculous haul some years before. Or perhaps it was the charcoal fire that Jesus had made to warm himself that took Peter back to the most painful memory of his life. Peter did not try walking on water as he had done that night when Jesus approached them across the sea: this time he plunged into the waves and swam to shore.

There were no recriminations or pleadings for forgiveness

in the poignant reunion of these two friends. Jesus simply asked Peter: do you love me? Three times Peter had denied knowing Jesus: now three times he was able to state, not only that he knew him, but that he loved him. This was a mature love founded on a real understanding of both himself and Jesus. Forgiveness is lavish with God. As in the story of the prodigal son whose father placed a gold ring on his finger, Jesus placed unlimited trust in Peter: 'Feed my sheep,' he said, as he re-commissioned Peter to care for his followers. Competence, experience and unblemished character were not qualifications. The central question for Jesus was only this: do you love me? It is the question he asks us.

It is interesting to speculate what might have happened had Peter answered 'Yes' instead of 'No' to the servant girl's allegation in the High Priest's courtyard. Had Peter been crucified alongside Jesus, the Christian Church might have been built on Paul's intellectual rigour or on James' authority. Instead it was built on Peter's love. We are told that, of faith, hope and love, the greatest is love: everything else will fade away. Peter's preaching, his sins, his leadership and martyrdom, even Peter's miracles – for he became the most famous miracle-worker of all the apostles – would one day be forgotten, but the love that plunged him into the Sea of Galilee will hold up the Church for ever.

There is a chilling postscript to the story of Peter's rehabilitation. When he left the High Priest's courtyard on that fateful night, Peter turned his back on suffering. In the lakeside reunion of a few weeks later the resurrected Jesus hinted that Peter would one day face a re-play of the scene he had avoided. 'When you are old,' he said, 'you will stretch out your hands and someone else will bind you and take you where you don't want to go' (John 21.18). Peter is thought to have gone to his own crucifixion in the persecutions of Nero's reign. Tradition tells us that Peter, who once blustered that he would be ready to follow Jesus to death, came to realize how unworthy he was to share the martyrdom of his Lord . . . and he asked to be crucified upside down.

Personal Reflection Time

➢ Is my behaviour sufficiently Christ-like for people to accuse *me* of being a follower of Jesus?

➢ Cock-crow signalled Peter's self-awakening. What has been my wake-up call? What fresh start might I want to make?

➢ Imagine Jesus turning to look at you. Respond to him in whatever way you want to.

Prayer

Though I follow at a distance
You know that I love you.

Though I have lied many times
You know that I love you.

Though I avoid your eyes of truth
You know that I love you.

Though I turn away from suffering
You know that I love you.

I hear the sounds of a new day
**Lord, you know everything;
You know that I love you.**

We remember before God . . .

- Prisoners of conscience

- Prisoners on death row

- Prisoners' families

Activities to Consider

❖ Write a letter in support of a prisoner of conscience. Amnesty International can give information about how to do this: www.amnesty.org.uk.

❖ Try rising early enough, especially if it is spring or early summer, to hear the dawn chorus. Let it be your act of worship.

❖ Be more aware of the way you look at people. Make an effort today to convey acceptance and understanding.

15

Within reach

... of the adoring

John 20.11–18

Mary stood crying outside the tomb. While she was still
crying, she bent over and looked in the tomb and saw two
angels there dressed in white, sitting where the body of Jesus
had been, one at the head and the other at the feet. 'Woman,
why are you crying?' they asked her.

She answered, 'They have taken my Lord away, and I do
not know where they have put him!'

Then she turned round and saw Jesus standing there; but
she did not know that it was Jesus. 'Woman, why are you cry-
ing?' Jesus asked her. 'Who is it that you are looking for?'

She thought he was the gardener, so she said to him, 'If
you took him away, sir, tell me where you have put him, and
I will go and get him.'

Jesus said to her, 'Mary!'

She turned towards him and said in Hebrew, 'Rabboni!'
(This means 'Teacher.')

'Do not hold on to me,' Jesus told her, 'because I have not
yet gone back up to the Father. But go to my brothers and
tell them that I am returning to him who is my Father and
their Father, my God and their God.'

So Mary Magdalene went and told the disciples that she had seen the Lord and related to them what he had told her.

It was not possible, working as a prison chaplain, to be with inmates all day long. Access was limited during the time they were locked in their cells. Many men dreaded those times when the heavy door slammed shut, leaving them alone or incarcerated with another prisoner in a space that afforded no privacy. I felt very close to them at such times. I would 'love them through the door', though they could not see or hear me. Their ears were too assailed by noise and shouting to be aware of a nearby prayerful presence.

God is also closer than we think, though not being able to perceive him with our senses makes it hard for us to believe he is involved in our world. We all struggle within our bodily prisons, with what may seem like the 'hard labour' of our working lives and with loneliness or other people's annoying behaviours. God knows our pain and extends his unfailing compassion. His Spirit moves freely through the locked doors of our hearts, and across boundaries of space and time to be with us. Yet we are scarcely aware of it.

Jesus promised to be with us always through his Holy Spirit. He is with us in his Body, the Church, in sacrament, in creation, in the poor, within our hearts . . . and he has promised to come again. Yet it is difficult to comprehend the 'other-ness' of God except in terms of distance. Like Thomas, unless we can see and touch, we find it hard to trust that Jesus is alive or that God cares. Feelings are reliable guides to our inner world but they can get it very wrong in trying to interpret what goes on around us. Just because we *feel* God is far away does not mean that he actually is.

A sense of separation seems to be part of the human condition, a restlessness not seen in other animals, a sense of dissatisfaction that unites people of faith and no faith. Many try to fill the void with possessions, to distract themselves with busyness and entertainment, to dull the pain by drugs or by moving from relationship to relationship. People of faith recognize the nature of the emptiness. That tortured cry from the cross, 'I thirst', keeps ringing in our ears. As Christ turned his head away from the sponge that soldiers raised to his lips, we understand his 'thirst' to be that longing of human beings for their God. Nothing else, ultimately, will satisfy any of us.

The closer we are to God, the more keenly we long for his presence. For the Christian, that deep desire will never go away: it is a very holy desire, the Spirit's work within us. We are God's lovers. We do not want the pain of separation to ease: it reassures us that we belong to him and re-orientates us to that place at the centre of our being where we find peace in doing what God wills. As Jesus explained to his disciples the night before his death, though we are in the world, ultimately we do not belong to it. This is the paradox: longing and waiting while peaceful and trusting; losing every battle against sin and death yet always making new beginnings in sure hope of victory already won. As Nicodemus was slow to learn, we are flesh and blood; we are also born of the Spirit.

Mary Magdalene's encounter with Jesus on the morning of the resurrection is a powerful picture of this in-between state of the Christian believer. In her desperate longing and failure to recognize Jesus even when he was standing next to her, we are reminded of our own lifelong search for somebody already within reach. 'Why are you crying?' is a question Jesus asks of us all, for God is not absent, lost, aloof or missing. No one has taken him away from us. Jesus challenges our perception of what is real and stretches our sense of what may be possible.

In the calling of Mary Magdalene's name, Jesus reminds us that God never fails to recognize us, even if we do not recognize him. It may be that we are trying to make God in our own image or into an image that feels comfortable. That image must assimilate what we know of Jesus' zeal and his joy, his outspokenness, authority, and freedom of spirit. Jesus has not changed: what changes is our dawning realization that there is more to him than we will ever be able to comprehend or embrace. Whenever we close our minds, Jesus simply rolls the stone away and appears in a new guise to call our name.

Like Mary Magdalene, we need to relate in a less anxious way – to Jesus, as well as to each other. What alternative is there but to trust in the bonds of fidelity and the capacity of relationship to grow and change, even to survive physical separation? Our reaching out must be not to strengthen our grip on whatever it is we are afraid of losing, but beyond that towards the glorious realization of our own potential to be as God desires us to become. Jesus' final statement to Mary Magdalene, 'Do not hold on to me . . .' was not a rebuff or rejection so much as a call to faith. It was to reassure her of his – and her – ultimate and unconditional belonging in God. The Spirit of Jesus would be with her and with his other disciples always and everywhere as an intimate friend. We cannot see the Spirit any more than we can see the wind, but we can, as Jesus told Nicodemus, see its effects clearly enough. It is in our own lives that we will see them.

Reluctance to loosen our grasp on something more tangible is understandable given our histories. When we cannot instantly access our personal needs, a childish sense of abandonment overwhelms us. Perhaps deep down we remember how as babies our mother did not always appear on cue when we cried. Children who feel secure can play independently, explore their environment and interact confidently with other children, but few of us have ideal childhoods, and we may grow up unsure whether we are loved or lovable. Our adult relationships may continue to show anxiety and insecurity. We may be clingy and untrusting and, like Mary Magdalene, easily feel robbed: '. . . tell me where you have put him'. Like her, we may have already written a script of our future that jumps to fearful conclusions. We may project our disappointment with parental figures on to God, our heavenly Father. Like a small child lingering at its parent's knees, we may be fearful of exploring faith issues and feel so paralysed by our own sense of inadequacy that we cannot accept forgiveness or be the bearer of good news to others. We will always hanker after reassurances that we are loved, that we exist. This is not what resurrection life is all about.

Jesus' resurrection appearances were not meant to be a tantalizing glimpse of what we may not touch, but to expand the limits of human existence and draw us into the infinite dimension where God dwells. We are still on earth and not yet risen, but love takes us beyond the petty world of the instinctual self; faith helps us see much further than the limited horizons of eyesight and imagination. The Christian life can be a series of resurrection experiences long before we rise to fullness of life in heaven. Feeling loved, we are already revitalized; energized by his Spirit, we live to fulfil God's workmanship in the here and now. Content with 'enough' and with who we are, happiness is not really so elusive. When Jesus commands us to 'go . . . tell . . .', our faces should bear the 'good news'.

Resurrection life is an expansion of possibility, a call to generosity of living, a glorious 'becoming' of who we truly are. As Jesus explained to Mary Magdalene, we must go out and *be* Jesus in response to his commandment to love. If feelings are what matter, then doing the will of the Father will make Jesus feel close. It will certainly make Jesus seem close for the people to whom we minister. Jesus was encouraging Mary to act as he did, to speak in his name, to deliver his message, to offer his healing, and to obey his command. In Jesus' name, Mary Magdalene and her brothers could approach God as *their* God, his Father as *their* Father.

In this, Jesus is always one step ahead of us, drawing us on. While the women gathered to anoint his body, Jesus had already risen; while Mary Magdalene held on to his resurrected body, he was already preparing to ascend; while the apostles gazed up into the heavens, the Spirit of Jesus was descending in tongues of flame. Jesus is not hiding; he is waiting. One glorious day he will welcome us home to heaven . . . and he is within reach even now.

Personal Reflection Time

➤ Read the scripture passage aloud to make this a personal encounter with the risen Lord. Substitute 'I' or 'me' or your own name whenever the text says 'Mary', 'she' or 'her'. Notice your feelings.

➤ When have I felt really alive? What is that telling me?

➤ What life-giving changes might you want to make in your life? Talk to Jesus about your desires and about any obstacles that seem to stand in the way.

Prayer

In endings and beginnings
I have seen the Lord!

In losing and in finding
I have seen the Lord!

In letting go and moving on
I have seen the Lord!

In changing and in growing
I have seen the Lord!

In living with new meaning
I have seen the Lord!

We remember before God . . .

- Recovering addicts

- Released prisoners

- New believers

Activities to Consider

❖ Resolve to be the bearer of only good news today. Notice people's mood rising.

❖ If it is autumn, buy some bulbs and plant them. Put the container in a cool dark place, remembering to water regularly. When shoots begin to appear, bring it into the light and let the colour and fragrance enliven you.

❖ If it is springtime, make an Easter garden. You might like to involve children in this activity. Find a deep tray and fill it with sterile compost. Make a tomb using stones, with the entrance rolled away. Sprinkle grass seed and add small plants. Tend the garden and watch it develop. Place three wooden crosses, folded grave cloths, and some figures to represent Jesus, Mary, the angels, etc. Tell the story to the children, using the figures to re-enact the drama of the resurrection.